Peace in the Family

Peace in the Family

A Workbook of Ideas and Actions

by Lois Dorn

with Penni Eldredge-Martin

 Pantheon Books, New York

All rights reserved under International and Pan-
American Copyright Conventions. Published in the
United States by Pantheon Books, a division of
Random House, Inc., New York, and simultaneously
in Canada by Random House of Canada Limited,
Toronto.

Library of Congress Cataloging in Publication Data

Dorn, Lois, 1942–
    Peace in the family.

    Bibliography: p.
    1. Family life education.   2. Conflict of genera-
tions—Prevention.   3. Problem solving, Group.
4. Parenting.   5. Interpersonal relations.
6. Peace.   I. Eldredge-Martin, Penni.   II. Title.
HQ10.D67   1983   306.8′7   83-42823
ISBN 0-394-51980-9
ISBN 0-394-71580-2 (pbk.)

Design by Gina Davis

Manufactured in the United States of America

First Edition

The photographs on pages 9, 22, 34, 50, 57, 79, and
118 are by Jeri Drucker; photographs on pages 29,
65, 87, 91, 106, 129, 141, and 155 are by Kenneth P.
Miller; photographs on pages 40, 101, 147, and 149
are by Manfred Dorn; drawings on pages 15, 18,
and 94 are by Mimi Harrison.

To my family . . .

My husband, Manfred
My sons, Paul, Kurt, and Gregg
My parents, John and Elva Pond

Who expect and appreciate my best efforts,
and who strengthen and delight me with theirs

Contents

Acknowledgments

I give special thanks to . . .

Penni Eldredge-Martin, my jovial and energetic co-coordinator of the Nonviolence and Children Program for two years, for her fellowship and hard work in developing, interpreting, and teaching the principles of nonviolence; and particularly for her authorship of the chapters and activities in Part Two on intergenerational support and on problem solving and conflict resolution, and for the Annotated Bibliography.

Anne Toensmeier, workshop facilitator, support giver, and friend, for her clarity, dedication, and warmth, in sharing the message of Nonviolence and Children; especially for her contribution of the Meeting Facilitation section of Part Two.

Leland and Mary Martha Howe, and Ed and Nila Betof, who have made great contributions in the fields of humanistic education and values clarification and who, through their dedication, clear thinking, and dynamic and artful teaching, have been a support and inspiration to us.

Milly Daniel and Wendy Wolf, my editors, who through their insight and example have afforded me new understanding and sources of support, and Mary DeVellis, for a sensitive and highly intuitive copy-editing job.

The committee members of the Nonviolence and Children Program of the Friends Peace Committee of the Philadelphia Yearly Meeting of the Religious Society of Friends, who gave me, as their staff person, the opportunity, guidance, and support to work, learn, and grow in the spirit of affirmation.

Introduction

For many parents childraising today is an exhilarating experience; for others it is a terrifying one. Society's changes come at us so rapidly that we can barely keep pace with them. Many of the challenges of our children's sociological and technological world were not a part of our own growing up, and it is often difficult to relate to or evaluate them objectively. From New Math to computer science, from acid rock to punk rock, there is a continual pressure for parents to keep informed, to understand. Today's children impress us. They mature faster, accumulate skills and information sooner, and demand independence more insistently than we did as children. Parents in this fast-moving society are expected to assume a flexible posture, allowing for the rapidly changing times, the cumulative life experience and emotional tenor of each family member, the chemistry of the interacting personalities, and the problems, conflicts, and accomplishments that are individually and jointly encountered. The incorporation of all these elements into a well-balanced parenting style, a manageable, positive approach, is an enormous challenge.

As members of a society sociologically and geographically in transition, we are deprived of the communities of support that families and neighborhoods anchored in tradition once offered. Attitudes about bringing up children have changed drastically in the last few generations. For those of us who are parenting in the 1980s, our frame of reference covers a sweep from the restrictive "do as I say, not as I do" approach of our grandparents and possibly our own parents, to the freewheeling, permissive "do you own thing" ideology prevalent in the 1960s and 1970s. Many parents find it difficult to take a firm stance on discipline or guidance for their children. They are unsure of the balance between the rights and needs of children and the rights and needs of parents.

A phenomenon of our times is guaranteed, instant success, insured by do-it-yourself psychology. We are inundated by books, TV programs, and training courses promising "*the* right way" to parent. These methods add new dimension to the confusion. Which should we choose? Given the variety of techniques and the unique perspective, circumstances, and abilities of each child and parent, how can each of these parenting methods be *"the* right way"? Yet, unsure of their own capabilities, many parents do become zealous method converts. Many parents are afraid to trust their own intuitions, concluding that their spontaneous expressions of personal values and attitudes are inappropriate.

Parenting from the book, like cake from the box, may seem simpler and safer, but it raises some familiar questions: Who gets the credit or the blame for the results? If all goes well, is it the people or the method that is successful? If things don't work out, is it the method, the parents, or the children that failed? Does it make the best use of the abilities and resources at hand? Is it authentic?

Parenting, like all relationship building, must be learned. It makes good sense, while developing resources and confidence, to borrow tools and ideas from other, experienced sources; but, eager to learn what is new, we should not overlook what we already know. We have all been children. We have all formed opinions about good or bad parenting through what we ourselves have experienced and observed. Each one of us, parent and child, has a lifetime of insight and experience to share. We are rich in firsthand information. For families to utilize and enhance their existing assets—experience, insight, and love—requires faith and a welcoming attitude toward unexpected results. It takes time and involves searching and testing; but the final product is an authentic parent-child relationship based on mutual growth.

Parenting courses can offer valuable assistance to families. They can increase the understanding of certain developmental patterns of children; they can provide a place to explore ideas and stimulate new thinking about parenting; and they can give parents the feeling of not being alone in their earnest and sometimes perplexing efforts at nurturing children. Learning parenting techniques, however, can do harm if it masks or compromises basic personal values, if it becomes a crutch that allows intrinsic relationship-building capabilities to atrophy, or if it gets in the way of genuine sharing. The parent education movement denotes an important shift in society's thinking

2

about families in that it has changed the emphasis from crisis intervention to crisis prevention. But, to this end, parenting methods must not sacrifice individuality and creativity to achieve harmony.

There is no single "right" way to parent. Healthy relationships and values cannot and should not be rigidly systematized. Force fitting parents and children into stereotypical roles violates their individuality and their ability to develop and contribute fully to society. When rights are denied, self-esteem diminished, and potential undermined, people become both victims and students of personal violence.

By today's media standards the use of the word "violence" in this context may seem strong, but as the civil rights and women's movements have graphically illustrated, violence is not necessarily accompanied by physical pain or obvious destruction. It is often quiet, subtle, and pervasive. Discrimination and insensitivity have a profoundly destructive and self-perpetuating effect on human development. The outwardly imperceptible hurts inflicted by ridicule, indifference, and disparagement can be devastating. To counteract this, nurturing institutions, such as schools and parenting programs, must consciously resist and oppose systems and attitudes that even inadvertently use oppression, manipulation, stereotyping, or devaluation to meet goals of convenience, conformity, or control. Ideally parent-child relationships (like all other relationships) should demonstrate harmonious mutual growth through nonviolent interaction. It is out of a commitment to this principle that in 1973 the Nonviolence and Children Program of the Philadelphia Yearly Meeting of the Society of Friends (Quakers) focused its work on affirming and giving educational and emotional support to families.

Initiated in the early sixties in response to the involvement of young people in the civil unrest of that time, the Nonviolence and Children Program is philosophically based in the Society of Friends' testimony of striving for peace through nonviolent action. Since its inception the NVC program has been working primarily with students and teachers in public and private schools in the Philadelphia area, sharing evolving techniques of nonviolently resolving conflict, building community, and developing self-esteem. The effectiveness and popularity of the program led to residential training workshops, in which teachers could learn in depth with their peers and colleagues, where participants, in an ongoing support network, could share successes, setbacks, and new ideas as colearners and coeducators.

Recognizing that families are the first and most influential educational arena, parenting workshops were a logical next step for the program. Like the teacher workshops they centered on the principle of affirmation, a secular term that encompassed the Friends' concept of "reaching for that of God in every person." The steering group of the Nonviolence and Children Program joined with the staff in forming a working test model of a parent support group, meeting monthly to develop a process of exchange of communication and encouragement for parents; and in 1975 the NVC program secured funding for a four-year outreach program on parent support work.

The Parent Support Project began with a year-long study group aimed at researching the historical and sociological perspectives of the family, including the current trends in parenting education. The study group was made up of seven committee members, with various personal and professional involvements with children and families: several teachers, a children's writer, and a psychiatric nurse; four of the members were parents. We set out to understand more about aggression—what causes it and how to channel it creatively, toward nondestructive ends. We studied feelings and the effects of their suppression and expression. We discussed power in families— who has it and how it is used. We felt concerned that many parenting techniques seemed to set efficiency and the compliancy of children as the major goals. Our aim was finding ways to demonstrate how power within the family can be shared, illustrating the valuable contribution that children can make to the family process, and encouraging and supporting parents and children in prizing their own inherent wisdom and skills. We hoped to emphasize the forming of relationships that would mutually affirm and develop the best personal and spiritual resources of children and parents, and their community.

During the year that we met, the study/support group functioned much as a family would, developing a sense of community by working and playing together. Individual members were encouraged to bring their own skills to the leadership of the group. We shared the responsibility for the work to be done—reading, researching, reporting, and interpreting material about families. Working in teams of two, group members read and reported on books, and facilitated discussion on the sociology of the family and current childraising methods. We read from Rollo May, Urie Bronfenbrenner, Arlene Skolnick, Hannah Arendt, Rudolf Dreikurs, Haim Ginott, Thomas Gordon, and others. We studied Parent Effectiveness Training, Transactional Analysis, Reality Therapy, and Behavior Modification. We invited outside speakers to present views on aggression and on the changing roles of women, men, and the family. As a backdrop to our discussions, during the course of the year each group member took a portion of one session to tell his or her life story, sharing what it was like to have been a child, showing the way each had developed an individual perception of parenting roles and adult-child relationships. Between sessions we each kept a journal, recording insights and observations about relationships with children, and at each meeting time was given for members who wished to read to the group from the journals. We affirmed and celebrated each other. We laughed, cried, and grew together in spirit, knowledge, and self-confidence. We synthesized a message and a program of affirmation and support.

In 1976, building on the work of the study group, the Nonviolence and Children Program expanded its field of learning by offering parenting workshops, seminars, and intergenerational workshops to schools, day-care centers, religious and community groups. These workshops were aimed at helping people step back from their anxiety about being "good" parents, teachers, or friends, so that they could get a clearer view of their relationships with children. Each person was encouraged to discover which were the important questions to ask himself: What am I doing *right*? How do I function best? What do I need to learn? How can I grow along with the children? What can I learn from them?

The program worked with groups of parents, teen-agers, school faculties, and combined parent-teacher groups always asking questions about childhood, adult-child relationships, parenting and being parented. We offered ideas, invited new thinking, and listened for insights and different viewpoints—letting the theory develop from the wisdom and perceptions brought to it by the participants. Several subcommittee members set up parent support groups in their own communities, also experimenting with different methods of group process and trying out various educational techniques to stimulate creative thinking about parenting concerns.

This book is the product of the Nonviolence and Children Program's Parent Support Project, and represents the applied thinking gleaned from more than ten years of study and field work on nonviolent child nurturing. It can be used either as a workbook by an individual, a guide to doing the exercises and keeping a journal; or as a handbook for a support group, in which the same material would be experienced through a structured, affirmation-centered group process.

The early chapters of this book outline NVC's central belief in affirmation—and its corollary, support—as a key factor in the development of positive human relationships and personal growth. With this philosophy as a base, we go on to look at how people—adults and children alike—can incorporate the principles of affirmation and support in the processes of their daily lives: in communicating, choosing values, establishing rules systems, and solving problems.

The working function of this book is to help readers set up mechanisms for sorting out, seeking feedback on, and evaluating personal attitudes about building relationships, especially between parent and child. The exercises and methods described are intended to aid in evaluating parenting ideologies, and to assess the support an individual may need to define and follow through on a self-determined parenting style; but the principles of affirmation and support can and should be applied to all personal interactions—with family, friends, neighbors, coworkers, even strangers. Positive expectation and encouragement strengthen and enrich all relationships. The Nonviolence and Children Program's primary goal in preparing this book, however, is to offer support to people who nurture children. Supporting parents means helping them to think clearly and positively about themselves as people, and encouraging them to think as clearly and as positively about their children, who are people, too! Nurturing parents know and like themselves and apply their basic understanding about human nature to children in the same way that they do to adults.

Part One
The Peaceable Family:
Where Do I Apply?

1 Affirmation—acting upon the belief in the innate goodness and capability of every individual—is the central theme of the Non-violence and Children Program's concept of human nurturing and parent-child relationship building. Recognizing that all living things grow best in a positive environment, we believe that children and adults alike need motivating encouragement and cheerful reassurances of how well they are doing if they are to develop to their fullest potential. Affirmation begins with a belief in oneself as an adequate creative nurturer and is combined with a deep conviction that the potential for growth, strength, and beauty in those we nurture is unlimited. Putting these beliefs into action creates supportive settings and opportunities for personal growth.

Affirmation

Affirmation is the open and nonmanipulative expression of appreciation for an individual's intrinsic worth and infinite potential. It is looking for and acknowledging by word and action what is special about each person, presenting it as a fact, not to flatter or secure a particular behavior, but to give credit and encouragement. People need appreciation for what they are if they are to grow into what they can be.

In each of our lives there are special people who have a way of demonstrating their faith in us, who help us see the strength and potential in ourselves, who affirm us. When we think about the times and ways these people have touched our lives, we experience a renewed sense of self-worth. At a parent's meeting that I attended at a child-care center, the group discussed the concept of affirmation and then settled into pairs to share stories about a person who had affirmed them during their childhood. A treasured memory popped instantly into my mind, and I eagerly led off the sharing with my partner:

"My great-grandmother affirmed my independence; she taught me about faith. She always told me, 'One door closes and another door opens.' There was never any question in her mind about whether she, I, or anyone else would measure up to the challenge of a newly opened door. After her husband died and her children were on their own, Granny sold her house, disposed of her material possessions, and set out on a journey of faith. Trusting in the hospitality of family members, she would spend a few special years in one home and then gracefully move on to another. Her open acceptance of each of us as good and special in our own right made her a welcome addition wherever she went. Her expectations that people would respond to her with kindness and good intentions brought a remarkable response.

"I clearly remember the day she came to our house, telling my mother she would like to stay for a while. She didn't take up much room, she wasn't much bigger than her suitcase, and her needs were few. Her greatest contributions were her presence and the profound impact of her faith and good will. With great patience she taught us some of what she knew: the Bible, a myriad of hymns, and how to crochet. She was excited about everything we did, listening with interest to the daily review of our lives. Most of all she believed in us and encouraged our every effort. Granny actively affirmed herself and everyone around her. She taught me to believe in people, beginning with myself."

Who Needs Affirmation?

We never outgrow our need for affirmation; we just grow out of expecting it. Affirmation enables people to actualize their potential. Though affirmation is always deserved, it is not always easily accessible; it helps when we can learn how to confidently request it. It is not uncommon for a child who feels in need of some reassurance to ask, "Tell me again about the time you were sick and I helped you," or, "I want to hear about how the whole family came to see me when I was born, even Aunt Liz who came on a plane from far away." Grownups, too, need to be reminded of their unique worth and capability, and rightly and wisely might say to a person from whom they draw support, "I need to hear about what you see me doing especially well as a parent"; or they might simply say, "I'd like a hug!" When a person receives and can assimilate enough affirmation, he feels happy and self-assured. He can more easily reach out to meet the needs and demands of others and to approach conflict and compromise with a positive, confident, giving attitude.

Countering Put-Downs

The attitude of affirmation runs counter to much of what our culture teaches us is acceptable or stylish. An important aspect of affirmation is putting into words positive observations and assumptions about people. Unfortunately in our society it is often considered chic to be casually critical of others. Put-downs are used as a form of friendly conversation. Teasing and "cutting up" have become a tolerated form of expressing acceptance. Hurtful names like dummy, nut, and fool are often used as endearments. We find it easier to exchange insulting familiarities than to comfortably express or receive straightforward approval and admiration. Because we fear misinterpretation, we hold back from saying positive things to people. We are anxious not to appear too sticky sweet, personal, or overly involved. Fearing that we will inflate people's egos, we do not express delight or admiration for their personalities. As children grow up they get the impression that speaking as an adult means perfecting sarcasm and criticism.

An exercise called I Am Lovable and Capable (IALAC),[1] developed by Sidney Simon, can give a demonstration of the effects of put-downs. Parents and teachers should be aware that IALAC and the Headband Exercise (p. 19) may engender intense feelings. Sensitively handled, however, both these exercises can help children and adults understand how it feels to treat people in certain ways. To do this exercise one person pins a sheet of paper with the letters IALAC to his shirt. Group members imagine that the sign wearer is a child just coming down to breakfast or entering class in the morning. Members call out typical comments that the IALAC person might

---

[1] Sidney B. Simon, *I Am Loveable and Capable* (Niles, Ill.: Argus Communications, 1973), pp. 2–31.

hear: "Late again," "Your shirt is out," "Good morning!" Each time a put-down is made, the demonstrator tears off a piece of the "I Am Lovable and Capable" sign. When a "put-up" is given, a piece can be taped back on, but the rift or scar remains, as it does in one's self-image.

We get so much negative input that it is hard at times not to give in to harsh assessments and just stop trying; but hearing the positives can often bring forth a potential strength. This was true for Helen when it came to doing math. Intimidated by a fourth-grade teacher who ridiculed her because she did not know her multiplication tables, she went through the remainder of her school life believing that she could not do math. She adjusted her career goals to avoid her weak point. When she married, she accepted her husband's promise to handle all the financial matters as an indication of his love and understanding of her. Only when faced with a financial crisis did Helen realize that she had allowed her teacher's put-down to become an excuse for irresponsible behavior. Forced to learn to write checks, Helen began to balance the checkbook by counting on her fingers. When she wanted and was offered a job that involved keeping books, she accepted it, then ran directly to the store to buy a calculator. One day at a staff budget meeting, when her concern overran her anxieties, Helen plunged into a discussion of the financial struggle. A coworker she particularly respected responded with, "Helen, that's a very important point; you really think well about money." Helen was overjoyed to realize that it was true, and she felt inspired to confront her lack of basic math skills so that she could take a firm hold on her personal finances. An affirmation thoughtfully expressed and responsibly accepted cleared the way for new growth.

All people need and deserve to hear about what they do well and how they enrich life. They should be affirmed. Any homemaker would love to hear, "Your caring for us shows in the work you do here." Every young person would delight to know, "You are so full of enthusiasm, it makes me feel good when you are around." The newspaper delivery person might be surprised but pleased to be told, "You are always prompt with the paper. I appreciate your good service." Opportunities to affirm people are always present, and it is important that we learn to use them.

Creating affirmation silhouettes[2] is one activity that makes a celebration out of affirming someone. The exercise provides a safe setting in which people can affirm and be affirmed; and also produces a permanent record of a person's affirmed qualities. Have the person to be affirmed lie down on a large piece of wrapping or art paper or an old sheet, so that someone can carefully trace an outline around her. The owner of the silhouette then draws in her features and clothing (others may assist at her invitation). After carefully discussing the concept of affirmation, family, class, or support-group members gather around the silhouetted person to offer comments of appreciation, which are then recorded on the silhouette paper. Be absolute about the ground rule "No put-downs!"

---

[2] Adapted from the exercises "Body Tracing," Harold C. Wells and Jack Canfield, *One Hundred Ways to Enhance Self Concepts in the Classroom: A Handbook for Teachers and Parents* (Englewood Cliffs, N.J.: Prentice-Hall, 1976), p. 159, and "Body Drawings," Robert C. Hawley and Isabel Hawley, *Developing Human Potential: A Handbook of Activities for Personal and Social Growth* (Amherst, Mass.: ERA Press, 1975), p. 35. For additional activities using affirmation silhouettes, see pp. 153–54.

Allow ample time for thoughtful participation, and be sure that the affirmed person has the full attention of the group. An affirmation silhouette makes a wonderful gift as part of a birthday or other celebration gathering. If the affirmation silhouette is drawn on a sheet, using permanent markers or textile crayons, it can be turned into a wall hanging or put on the bed so that the owner can wrap herself up in love and appreciation.

Affirming Ourselves and Others

For most of us, affirming ourselves seems even more uncomfortable than affirming others. Trained to be modest and self-effacing, we automatically attack our own self-image. We deflect positive feedback, diminishing it with the claim, "It was nothing." If we are told that our clothes are tastefully chosen, we hastily point out how cheap or old they are. If we receive the compliment that we look attractive or that we are clever, rather than appear vain we call immediate attention to our most recent blooper or note how much more attractive or clever someone else is. It is unthinkable to reply with, "Yes, I'm delighted you noticed!" We victimize ourselves in a trap of pervasive humility, questioning, and worrying about our real worth. Floundering in insecurity, we send out signals that perhaps we are not as capable or lovable as might be wished. As people respond provisionally to our unsureness, our self-doubts gradually begin to be realized. In an attempt to bolster our own flagging self-image, we desperately focus on the shortcomings or vulnerabilities of others. Children who are not able to affirm themselves establish patterns of insecurity that often follow them through life. If they see themselves as inferior, they may choose to assume the role of victim, by constantly feeling or even allowing themselves to be picked on or by-passed; or they may compensate for their insecurity by attempting to victimize others, by bullying and undercutting them in order to feel powerful. When we do not feel confident of our own strength, goodness, or success, there seems to be comfort and reassurance in establishing that others are "less than" we are. This damaging downward spiral is one that affirmation can reverse.

Verbalizing one's own strengths and abilities is a first step toward taking responsibility for acting on them. Much of the process of learning and growing is getting past a negative self-image. It is difficult to risk doing or learning new things when you doubt that you've got what it takes to do it. It is frightening to expose the creative side of yourself when you fear that others might ridicule or scorn your efforts. It is impossible to believe in yourself and realize your full potential when what you hear from others, and what you tell yourself, is that you don't measure up. Affirming people (including ourselves) through a positive attitude reflected in our speech and actions counteracts society's glib undermining of self-esteem. Affirmation practices and projects the belief that people have infinite potential for good. Affirmation can reverse the downward spiral and generate new self-esteem, productivity, cooperation, and joy.

It is helpful to take stock now and then of our own affirmability. Creating a personal shield[3] is one way to illustrate our specialness. Draw the shape of a shield on a piece of paper. Divide the shield into four sections, and number each section. In each make a simple drawing to represent an area of personal pride: a happy occasion in your life; something you did that was difficult; a goal you have for yourself; something about you that people would miss if you weren't around. Beneath the shield write a motto you might be known for. Take a few minutes to explain your shield to a partner or a friend. Hang it up where you and others can see it, or keep it in your journal.[4] See one example on the following page.

---

[3] Adapted from the exercises "Personal Coat of Arms," Sidney B. Simon, Leland W. Howe, and Howard Kirschenbaum, *Values Clarification*, pp. 278–80 (see the Annotated Bibliography, p. 176), and "Personal Coat of Arms," Harold C. Wells and Jack Canfield, *One Hundred Ways to Enhance Self Concepts in the Classroom: A Handbook for Teachers and Parents* (Englewood Cliffs, N.J.: Prentice-Hall, 1976), p. 51.
[4] For an explanation of how to keep a journal, see p. 131.

Beyond Praise and Criticism

The attitude of affirmation brings a more positive direction to our use of praise and criticism. Affirmation involves giving thoughtful, informative feedback about a person's capability. Unlike praise or adulation, it is never intended to flatter or manipulate. Though affirmation often gives information that supports and encourages change, unlike criticism it never ridicules or condemns. Affirmation never questions the ultimate worth of individuals. It is not expressed in absolute terms of good or bad. Affirmation provides information that encourages and demonstrates the belief in personal growth.

Too often praise is used to manipulate or control behavior: "Mommy's good boy mustn't get dirty"; "Be a nice girl and show Aunt Mae how beautifully you play the piano"; or, "You're such a good friend, I know you'll never tell." Flattery, like a sugar high, gives a momentary uplift that gives way quickly to anxiety. The receiver is left to worry: "Would they still like me so much if I behaved differently?" It is difficult, especially for children, to think of behavior as separate from self. Carelessly used praise and criticism can lend credence to reasoning such as, "I am being quiet—I am good"; "I spilled my milk—I am bad." Affirmation emphasizes the belief that through the variations of behavior a person's goodness and worthiness remain constant. Praise and criticism can put the lid on expanding talents, allowing a person to conclude, "I'm a lost cause, no use trying"; or, "I'm already doing the best that can be expected of me, there is no point in working harder."

Affirmation is not just stroking or saying positive things. Often it expresses what needs to be changed, but does so in a tactful, informative way: "Joe, you have a quick and insightful wit. Sometimes, though, people dismiss the important points you make because they think you are just kidding. I think your views deserve to be taken more seriously at times." Affirmation is not just acknowledging what is, but asserting what can be. When based in affirmation, evaluative information is not constructive criticism; nor does it shame or intimidate. Affirmation encourages observing and focusing on cultivable strengths rather than classifying undeveloped strengths as weaknesses. It shows interest and involvement. It emphasizes support: "You are important to me. I think about and appreciate you."

Positive Expectations

Faith, or positive expectation, is at the heart of the concept of affirmation. In an affirming relationship, interactions reflect trust and an expectation of continuing growth. The Headband Exercise[5] demonstrates how expectations about an individual affect behavior. In this exercise each person in the group receives a headband that is labeled with a stereotypical behavior: "Organizer," "Know It All," "Crybaby," etc. The wearer has no idea what the label says. As the group mingles and interacts, responding in accordance with the label each person bears, there are interesting shifts in behavior. An

---

[5] Learned from Erline Sloane, Affective Education Department, Philadelphia Board of Education.

ordinarily passive person, labeled and reacted to as a bully, may assume a newly assertive posture in response to the hostility or fear that he encounters. Vacillators or agitators, addressed as trusted leaders, may be induced to take on the roles of decision makers and mentors. People act out the roles cued to them by others' expectations. Negative suppositions about ability or motivation diminish self-esteem and performance. Positive expectations and a supportive approach encourage a cooperative, self-assured response. Certainly a child is bound to feel more willing and capable when cheerfully invited, "Let's clean up your toys now," than if challenged, "You are a mess! Can't you even help clean up after yourself?" The temporary shifts in behavior witnessed in the Headband Exercise suggest what could happen if people were always treated with respect and positive expectation.

Remembering the moments when others have believed in us (perhaps even more than we believed in ourselves) can bolster our confidence and help us to do our best. Marlene, now a mother herself, still remembers vividly how being trusted as a child helped her grow:

"When I was little we were very poor. One day my mother was sick, and she gave me the little bit of money she had and told me to go to the store for groceries for the family. We lived a long way from the store and I had never gone alone before. I was afraid I would lose the money. I was pretty small, and the groceries were very heavy because of the potatoes. I felt so proud when I got home. I never forgot how Mama trusted me."

Acting on the Belief

Action is the most important dimension of affirmation. The family setting provides many opportunities for children's developing strengths to be tried; it is a place where children can take risks and grow. But, in part because of a loving wish to take care of our young, and also because of external social pressure to fill a prescribed parental role, parents often impede children's development by not putting their affirming belief in them into action. Pressed to feel personally accountable for all their children's acts, it is understandable that parents are often apprehensive about allowing children new opportunities. To a child who innocently pulls out the bottom box of a cereal display, the results may be as pure and wondrous as those of Galileo's experiments with tumbling weights at Pisa, but for that child's parent, it may more likely become a public humiliation: he might only hope to disappear into thin air, leaving behind a well-noted, "I taught her better than that!" Wanting things to run smoothly, without casualty or embarrassment, we sometimes excessively restrict children or do for them what they could more beneficially do for themselves. For "their own good" (and for our parental image) we fence children in. We stuff them into shopping cart seats or hold them on verbal leashes of "Don't touch!" or "No! No!" rather than take the time and risks necessary to help them learn through experiencing.

Because they feel required to assume the role of total caretaker, many parents push themselves to superhuman extremes, shortchanging themselves and underestimating their children. "When I was first divorced," a member of a support group shared, "it was difficult not having someone else to help with the work and responsibilities. I worked all day and still had to come home at night to take care of the house and my four-year-old daughter. By the end of the day I was exhausted. One night I flopped down on the sofa before dinner and fell asleep. When I woke up I found that my daughter had made us turkey sandwiches for dinner. The mayonnaise was about an inch thick and there was hardly any turkey, but it was great. She was showing me that she could help. It's really wonderful to know that the world doesn't fall apart when you don't do everything for your kids. She and I both felt good about it. Since then I count on her to help me with the cooking. I enjoy the company, and she knows she is really important."

The challenge for parents and children is to discern, instance by instance, the shifting boundaries of restriction, support, and autonomy; to push aside stereotypical expectations about what "good" parents and "good" children do; and to find a balance between

restraint and release that allows children to learn safely from their actions while parents confidently lend support.

This balancing of children's and parent's needs can be illustrated in another way by considering the practice of playpenning young children. Without a doubt a playpen provides a certain amount of safety, particularly when an adult cannot be present to watch for and teach about hazards. It also provides a safe setting in which a child can learn to spend time playing without depending on another person. If a child spends all his time in a playpen, however, he will not encounter or learn to recognize the pleasures and dangers of his broader environment. And while he may develop some appreciation for solitude and independent play within the confines of his pen, his need to learn and practice the skills of social interaction through playing and dealing with others may not be realized.

Children need to be protected and guided, but they also require the freedom to learn how to protect and guide themselves. Even as children mature, some parents may habitually pen them within intellectual and experiential boundaries. Putting barriers between children and their peer culture, restricting their access to reliable information about issues that might concern them—religion, politics, sex, or drugs—and denying their ability to act independently often leave them unprepared to make informed decisions. The safety gained is temporary at best, and the lack of valuable practice in decision making may become a liability to the young person in the long run. Holding children too close is a dangerous disservice, and it negates the proposition that children can learn to make responsible judgments. When a person is affirmed for his potential or developing strengths but denied opportunities to act on them in a meaningful way, real conflict can arise. Children striving to become independent and self-directed are confused and frustrated by a parent who clings too tightly to the reins of power. It is unfair to everyone to expect children to grow up yet not let them. As parents, we affirm ourselves and our children best when we support them in developing and acting on their capabilities.

Involved Trust

Affirmation does not entail abandonment. Allowing children to race up and down supermarket aisles using the baskets as go-carts is not a way of showing trust. It indicates disinterest or an assumption that children cannot or will not behave reasonably. Affirmation is not permissiveness, but involved trust. A child old enough to walk safely up and down the supermarket aisles, who is busy with the task of finding assigned items, is not only developing motor coordination, reading ability, problem-solving competence (when he can't reach something), and social and communication skills (should he decide to ask for assistance), but he also has a real sense of being a trusted family contributor. This child gains admiration and respect, and his parents receive some valuable assistance. Both the relationship and the individuals are assertively affirmed.

Involved trust requires combining belief in ability with a willingness to assist when needed; giving time, information, and resources is part of affirming a person. A child who is failing algebra needs more than a "I know you can do it!"—he needs someone to show him how it is done. Children need encouragement, support, and the availability of an involved person who will underscore successes, encourage continuing effort, and render information and assistance when it is needed.

Affirming Ourselves as Parents

Far more than mere figureheads, parents must recognize themselves as valuable resources to children. As parents we need to affirm the importance of our own life experiences as priceless sources of insight and information that we can share with our children; we should assert what we believe and know, in a positive way. In the same way, we must affirm our children and our relationships with them by acknowledging and encouraging these same developing resources of insight and information within them. Remembering that each person and every relationship is unique, we must approach parent-child relationships with the respect, self-assuredness, and enthusiasm of pioneers, and must seek to appreciate our resourceful use of skills, intuition, and knowledge in meeting the challenge of a new adventure.

2 Families have special needs for affirmative support. Just as children need encouragement and assistance to feel secure in risking new ways of thinking and acting, parents also in a learn-as-you-go role need the assurance of available sources of active support. For every parent "now" seems like the most difficult time to parent. Changing social dynamics aside, whenever you are parenting, it takes on an urgency and uniqueness because *you* are doing it and *your* children are experiencing it! Parenthood, like childhood, is a relationship in which vulnerability is maximized. It is a deeply emotional, intensely involved, creative investment of self. It is a time of perpetual on-site training, when self-doubts often soar and feelings of adequacy and worthiness sometimes plummet. Parents, as well as their children, have an enormous need for nurturing support.

The Art of Giving and Receiving Support

Affirmation involves giving and receiving nurturing support. Acting on the belief that each person is innately and immeasurably capable, nurturing support makes available to another those abilities, resources, and reassurances that will free or aid that person to utilize and develop fully his own skills and responses. Growth-enhancing support must be carefully tempered to give a sense of reinforcement, while calling forth the supported person's unique insights and strengths. Nurturing support must be given and asked for only to the extent that it is truly needed, and should be done so in a way that encourages and credits individuals with the ability to grow in resourcefulness, skill, and responsibility.

Individual interpretation drastically alters the concept of giving support and the level of expectation in seeking it. For some people, supporting someone means providing for all their needs. For others, supporting means cheering someone on, with perhaps no commitment to supply any tangible assistance. Throughout society we can see examples of systems that claim to support people when in actuality they dominate or subjugate them. Nurturing support never diminishes a person's sense of self-worth or arrests learning or skills development. Affirming support provides reinforcement that enables personal growth.

As an assistant teacher in a Montessori nursery school, I learned some important lessons about defining the limits of nurturing support. I had originally been drawn to the Montessori method of education for my own children because of its respectful, self-directed approach, its premise that learning belongs to the child and that adults should observe and guide but never intrude on the process. It was through working in the classroom, though, that I really began to understand the importance of discerning and honoring the sometimes vaguely defined border between interference and support.

Learning to put coats on, one of the first tasks set for children at our school, symbolized new freedom to them; but for me, as teacher, it became an illustration of the true quality but changing form of nurturing support. To put on a coat by himself, the child spreads it out on the floor with the arms outstretched and the front sides open. Standing behind the collar edge of the coat, the child slides his hands into the sleeves, flips the coat over his head, and *voila!* the coat is on. Simple as this sounds and is, many children, by standing at the wrong edge of the coat, literally strait jacket themselves in their attempt at independence. Those children who caught on to the technique immediately would often demonstrate their new discovery matter-of-factly to the others, but, as peers, they seemed neither tempted, nor were they expected, to take over the job for their friends. As an adult, my role as a support person was harder to maintain. Frustrated children saw me as someone who could "do it" for them, and their poignant pleas fell on compassionate ears. With pressing time schedules and noontime stomachs roaring to be fed, the temptation to put their coats on for them was enormous, but doing so would have kept them dependent. My job was to remain close by, cheerfully and believingly encouraging all efforts. At times it was necessary to give clues, such as, "I think it will work better if you stand on the side where the collar is," or to offer reinforcing information: "Would you like me to show you again how it works?"

One child who grew very special to me seemed completely stymied by the coat trick. Cari was an awkward little girl with a chronically runny nose, damp pants, and a whiny voice. Her mother laughingly called her Klutz and compared her unflatteringly to an older, more accomplished sister. In the mother's exasperation and embarrassment about Cari's slowness, she had chosen to do everything for her. Cari, however, never gave up the belief that she could do it herself. No matter what the challenge, she steadfastly maintained, "I want to . . . I can . . . I will do it myself!" Cari and I spent a lot of time together in that coat room. While she learned about putting on coats, I learned about determination and self-esteem. The only support Cari allowed or needed was a caring presence, a tiny bit of information, and a chance to think. For most of the children, learning to put on their coats was an exciting trick, but for Cari, when the moment came, it was a jubilant personal victory. Because we had been able to carefully work out the limits of support, she truly owned her success.

Getting Support

As evolving contributors to our personal and world community, we have an obligation to get the support that will help us become our own best self. The more we grow the more we will be able to reinvest. As we seek to avail ourselves of trustworthy support, as we develop and utilize our own skills, we become better able to give support to others who are also striving to grow. The more independent we become the more wholesomely interdependent we can be.

In seeking nurturing support we must start by evaluating what our specific needs are, then assess and affirm our own resources that are available to meet them. Beginning with the question "What talents, insights, and skills do I have that I can draw on?" we decide what we can do or learn to do for ourselves. We must be truthful but generous and affirming in this assessment. Next we must ask, "What other help is needed, and who might be able to provide it?" In this case we not only turn our affirming appraisal to consider those who generally support us, but extend it to consider new resources in our personal community of support. Again we must not underestimate either ability or willingness but give people a chance to decide and say for themselves what they can or cannot give. Once we determine the kind of additional support that may be necessary and identify those who might best supply it, it is our responsibility to seek that vital support actively, asking for it repeatedly if necessary, or, if it is not available from one source, seeking it from someone else. When we conscientiously pursue support in this way, affirming and drawing on ourselves as the primary source of strength and action, it can then be accepted confidently and with pleasure when we receive it.

All of us experience times when no one offers us support. We may feel as though we shouldn't have to ask for it: "If she really cared she'd know what I need." This is a grossly unfair expectation. No one can know exactly how you feel or what you need, for no one else is you! No matter how familiar a person may be, he cannot possibly know exactly what we are thinking, because each of us experiences life uniquely, from our own point of view, and our perceptions are constantly changing. The fact is that aside from those very rare times when someone intuitively offers the support that is just what we need, we must most often specify it. Young children can communicate their need for support even before they are able to talk—by crying and fretting, or by acting fearful, frustrated, or listless. The task of identifying the need and determining the appropriate support, in this case, falls largely on the support-giving person.

As people mature they are expected to accurately define and acceptably express their needs for support; but the fear of rejection or feelings of pride and independence can get in the way of doing so. When we need support, it is important to remember that requesting what we need affirms us (I deserve this help) and, at the same time, affirms those we ask it of (I recognize you as a valuable resource in this situation, as someone I can trust with my vulnerability). People enjoy giving when they can, especially if the assistance has clear perimeters and is received graciously and with pleasure. Learning to ask for necessary encouragement is a step toward developing relationships in which support is freely given and received.

Each of us has particular qualities or strengths that are valuable in offering support. We all benefit from and can contribute importantly to individual support networks. Taking stock of our support resources gives us a chance to affirm our own and others' special supportive abilities and may show us where new support links need to be developed. To get a quick overview of your support network, draw up a Support Balance Sheet:

Draw a line down the center of a piece of paper. Down the right side list those people who turn to you for support. Note next to each name the type of support that is usually requested of you. Down the left side of the paper list those people you feel you can call on for support. Next to each name indicate the type of support each person can be counted on to supply. With a partner take turns sharing how

you view your balance of support. Affirm and record your particular support-giving strengths. What other kinds of support would you like to have available to you? Include the balance sheet in your journal, and update it from time to time. Remember, needs and strengths change.

Specific support must be defined and requested if we truly hope to get it. Perhaps we need some attentive listening while we talk a problem through, or a ride to the doctor, or someone to take care of the children while we clear our mind. We must be specific about what we need and pursue it without apology. Asking for support helps us to define our needs. Explaining our problem pushes us to sort through the emotions attached to the situation, and to determine which feelings can lead the way to action. Articulating a felt need gives it form, sometimes a surprisingly unexpected one. We may discover a hidden need (having my husband care about sharing the housework) beneath the surface need (getting him to help clear the table). Once the real issue is uncovered, it may change the initial

SUPPORT BALANCE SHEET

I go to . . . . . for		. . . . . comes to me for	
Jane	a good cry	Barb	listening, babysitting
Mike	hugs	Mary	affection, advice talking things
Mom	listening	Mike	through

1) I can give . . . . . good attention.
2) I need . . . . . someone to laugh with.

goal or request. We may start out thinking, "I'm not able to do this —someone will have to help me," but given the chance to state the need and the feelings that accompany it, we may discover that support was not necessary at all, only the opportunity to confront the feelings.

Though we all deserve and need support, we often find it difficult to ask for it. We get confusing signals from people about the acceptability of seeking it. On the one hand, it is implied that we should not be too proud to accept assistance, but on the other, we know that there is a stigma to being needy or seeming weak. We are encouraged to enjoy, share, and be open about our lives, but in the face of difficulties we are also expected to maintain our dignity and not burden others with our problems. Often our own self-doubts, feelings of embarrassment, unworthiness, or fear of being refused are barriers to getting support. We feel unsure of what we can expect to have accepted as a legitimate and reasonable request.

Remembering that support should be an amplification of our own strengths and efforts, we have the right and the obligation to ask for exactly (but only) what we genuinely need to act responsibly. For instance, Carol, the divorced mother of six-year-old David, is feeling tied down. Her outside employment, household chores, and job as a parent leave little time for a social life, and there is no money for a baby-sitter. Carol is getting physically and emotionally run-down and is beginning to take her frustration out on David. She feels and acts cranky and resentful when she is with David and with growing frequency sends him off to bed for minor indiscretions. Carol has an obligation to herself and to David to break out of this negative situation. She needs to seek support from a family member or a friend: perhaps she could trade some seedlings from her garden or half of her next big batch of spaghetti sauce for some free child care while she makes the time to do something nice for herself. After Carol affirms herself for what she is already doing well, and carefully assesses what she needs and what she can contribute toward it, asking for the additional support will then demonstrate her clear thinking and sense of responsibility.

It is essential to ask for support open-endedly, acknowledging that if a person says no it does not mean that we have been personally rejected or that the person asked is inadequate in any way; but that in a quest for effective support, this person may not be the best resource right now. When this happens we can appreciatively and self-assuredly ask again from others until we get what we need. Although a person may tell us no, he can still affirm us as capable, resourceful, and responsible people; able to respond positively to his decision and capable of acquiring the needed support from other sources. Similarly, when we are offered support that we do not need and that will diminish our efforts toward self-actualization, we can and should say, "Thank you, but no. It is important to me to do that myself."

Giving Support

Throughout our lives we all benefit from giving as well as receiving support. Since there is goodness and capability in every person, support is available from every one of us! There is not an "in group" who does it the right way and an "out group" who does it wrong. Although some problems or situations may require professional attention, all people have the ability to be a resource to others.

Just as with asking for support, there is a continuum that we should follow in giving it, too. First, we should think carefully and affirmingly about ourselves as support givers and about the people we will offer support to; it is necessary to assess thoughtfully what we may be needed to do, and what we feel able to offer. Next, we tentatively offer the support that seems right: it may involve listening, accepting the expression of feelings, supplying information, practical assistance, or feedback. If we are asked for support and are able to provide it, we should remember to give just what is asked for. If we cannot help, we should say so, perhaps suggesting others who can be a resource. Finally, our efforts should be aimed toward anticipating, encouraging, and celebrating autonomous growth and decreasing dependency.

Accepting Feelings

At times, affirming a person who feels pressured or inadequate in the face of difficulty will release a flood of doubts, fears, and misgivings. As a support giver it is important to remember that all of these feelings have real meaning for their owner. The best support is to allow the feelings to be expressed. This emptying out, like the pouring out of grief, can make room for new feelings of hope, self-appreciation, and determination. This was the result when Barbara provided accepting, affirming support to her friend Esther during a crisis.

Esther, the mother of a lively sixteen-year-old, Jeanie, was stunned when she received a call from a local department store, informing her that Jeanie had been caught with some of her friends shoplifting stereo tapes. Distraught and confused, Esther stopped at Barbara's house, explaining, "I'm on my way to pick Jeanie up. She's gotten in some trouble. Before I go there I need to get a hold of myself. Can you give me a little time and just listen?"

Esther poured out her pain, shock, and rage, while Barbara listened quietly and attentively, making no judgments. She offered no suggestions or condolences but gave her full attention to her friend.

"How could she do this? She knows better! I have taught her better!" Esther railed. "What will people think?"

"You are worried that people will think badly of Jeanie and you," Barbara said softly. "You feel embarrassed."

"I feel so angry and afraid!" Esther sobbed. She covered her face and let the tears flow while Barbara held her gently. When her tears subsided, Esther said resolutely, "I don't know what happened today, but I do know that I believe in Jeanie and I love her. That is the first thing I'm going to make clear when I walk into that office. Jeanie needs and deserves my support, and together we can work this through."

Expressing and accepting feelings is an important part of confronting problems. We affirm and support people when we offer a caring and respectful audience for their feelings.

Listening

Attentive listening is an essential part of providing affirmative support. In addition to allowing feelings to flow, it implies trust in a person's ability to produce well-suited answers to her own problems. A good listener provides a safe opportunity for rational sorting out and sounding out, and gives feedback only when it is welcome. A person who listens with caring interest can encourage a problem solver to express and expand her insights and ideas for action. When it becomes necessary to release feelings and so move toward new answers, a person who can listen without agreeing, denying, or judging is not only a comfort but, by her presence, a reassuring reminder of how valuable the problem solver herself is.

John puts his listening skills to work in his job as an office coordinator. He is supportive of his coworkers by offering them informal opportunities to sort out dissatisfactions or worries without judgment or consequences attached. Intuitively he seems to pop up at just the right moment with an open invitation to listen. "What's happening?

Want to go for a walk or get a cup of coffee?" are his clues that if you need a sounding board or just someone to be with, he is available. It is safe to talk things out in John's presence, because he is careful not to give advice or lead the conversation. If he has a view to contribute, he puts it in terms of, "One thing that I've tried is . . ." or, "Have you thought about . . .?" Most important, it is clear that he is not snooping, since he never asks probing questions or gossips about what he hears. Once you've had your say, it is as if the conversation never happened, except perhaps for an occasional encouraging smile or a light but caring, "How are things going?"

Careful listening should be an ongoing kind of support, not saved only for crises. By showing interest and encouragement in a steady, quiet way, we give a sense of support that can be assimilated so as to enhance a person's self-esteem. This sense of security then becomes a part of him; it springs from the knowledge that support is always available to him. This kind of affirmation—demonstrated in simple ways, such as providing the time and attention for sharing the experiences of the day when the family congregates each evening, or making a phone call, or sending a note to a friend just to say hello—creates an awareness of affirmation: "I am important, people care about me."

Sharing Resources

Many times support is needed in a more tangible form. It may be necessary to provide particular services or skills to help a person accomplish what needs to be done such as trading baby-sitting time so that parents can run an errand, go to school, or have some time for themselves. It might be helping a friend wallpaper a room or lending the tools necessary to do the job. Jack and his friend Sid often exchange help with household repairs. In addition to lightening the work load, these exchanges not only provide an opportunity for the sharing of ideas and experiences but also give them the pleasure of a gratifying companionship. Another way of giving practical help is by sharing information. If someone is lacking expertise in a particular area, a support person, rather than jumping in to take over the task, can help by providing information that will enable the person to feel confident in that area. We do this when we teach children the steps in making their own simple meals, cleaning their rooms, or negotiating a purchase. We should also use this teach-and-release approach when we support adults who need to know *how* to do something, but not have it done for them.

Letting Go

In giving support to others we must not only acknowledge their present strengths but should recognize and whenever possible encourage them to develop new dimensions of self-help. One school principal showed this kind of support by giving the ultimate choice of resolutions to the person who would be most deeply affected by it. After interviewing separately an academically struggling newcomer to the school and his parents, the principal carefully outlined *to the boy* the possible options available to him:

"Paul, you have been having a very difficult time with some of your studies. I want you to have a good learning experience here. As I see it, you have three choices. All of them have some happy and some unpleasant consequences attached. First, you can choose to go on to the eighth grade and get some tutoring to help you catch up. I know that you are an excellent athlete and realize that it might be hard for you to give up after-school sports for tutoring. Second, you could choose to go to summer school and get special attention in the subjects in which you need more skills. However, after a difficult year, you may feel that you need a break from school and may want to go on to summer camp as you had planned. Third, you might choose to re-enter seventh grade this fall and get a fresh start on the material, but in some ways you may feel uncomfortable about repeating a grade, and you may even have to put up with some teasing about it from the other children. I hope you will think carefully about the benefits and difficulties of all these choices. We are prepared to work with you on whichever of these plans you feel you can make a commitment to, but you are the best judge of what will be the most workable solution for you."

Later Paul reported matter-of-factly to his parents that he had decided to repeat seventh grade. Mom and Dad, who had resisted pressure from Paul's former school to "hold him back," were amazed.

"It's okay, I didn't get left back." Paul cheerfully assured them. "I know that I need the help. I'm not ready to go on to new stuff, and I made the choice myself!"

The principal had credited Paul with knowing his own emotional needs best. He had given all the information he could, simply, both pro and con, and then had trusted Paul to make the decision that he could live and work with most comfortably. Affirmed for his inherent good judgment, and supported in taking an important first step in assuming responsibility for his own progress, Paul felt pride in and commitment to *his own* difficult decision.

THE ART OF GIVING AND RECEIVING SUPPORT

Honoring Limits

Whatever the type or amount of support given, it is important that it not exceed what is actually needed. The giver and receiver must agree in their view of appropriate support. It is essential to match the support exactly to what the receiver needs, wants, and can accept. My friend Anne is terrific at gauging which kind of support would be most helpful. One year, worn out by a self-imposed, frenzied schedule, I became anemic. Caught between lethargy and my compulsion not to give in, instead of resting I pushed myself harder and harder. I felt annoyed with myself, and though I couldn't hide my ill health and depression, I also couldn't bear to let anyone take over for me. Anne checked very carefully to see what kind of help I could accept.

"Do you want to send the boys up here for a few days, or can I do some shopping for you?"

"No thanks, we're doing fine," I chirped. I could not publicly admit that I was running out of steam as super mother.

"Okay, well, just remember that I love you," Anne replied, and changed the subject.

The next day Anne arrived at my house for a committee meeting armed with a molasses-fortified gingerbread, a bowl of fresh applesauce, and a big hug. I felt loved and firmly reminded of how important my health is, to me and to those around me. After a good laugh, we talked about nutrition, schedules, and health. The talk was wonderful medicine in itself, and by the time Anne left, I was happily aware of what I needed to do. I was on the road to recovery thanks to Anne's insightful matching of support to needs.

Saying No

An important part of giving appropriate support is saying no. Although everyone does have the potential to give support, anyone may, for a number of good reasons, be unable at times to give the support asked for or needed. No one should have to give at her own emotional or physical expense. It is important to say no when we do not have the patience, emotional energy, time, or health to give the support requested. If possible, at these times we might try to refer the asker to someone who can help. At other times, when we are asked for help but clearly feel that the asker is able to help himself and would be better aided by doing the task on his own— as with the children putting on their coats—it is again important to say no. After giving the assurance that our emotional and moral support is solidly there, it is sometimes most affirming to say, ''You can do this better than I.''

Though giving support is a mutually enriching experience and makes us, as givers, feel good and pleased with ourselves, we must always be mindful not to make others dependent on our support. We need to find the balance between what we are able and willing to give, and what others can supply, and are best served by supplying, themselves. The most rewarding moment for a support giver should be when the person he has supported can stand on his own. The goal of support is to assist others in becoming autonomous. Certainly our aim is not to do without others, but rather to motivate people toward realizing their potential so that they and we are enriched.

Parent Support Groups

One place in which people can think about and learn new support skills is in support groups. The support group provides the opportunity for people to look at what they need, consider what hinders them from getting it, and discover what resources are available within themselves and from others in their communities. In a support group people can experience and practice affirming support.

Though we don't call them by that name, each of us is already a member of a number of support groups: family, friends, community, church, and so on. When these home-base groups are anchored in a spirit of affirmation, we learn about ourselves and others, exchange and develop ideas and skills, and find the kind of attention that gives us comfort and encouragement. As one mother put it:

"I believe that most of what I do now, as a mother and as a child-care person, is related to the support I received from La Leche League, from my neighbor (four years my junior but ahead of me as a mother), and from a system of networking that I just fell into as a way of life in the past several years. As a mother, whenever there was a void in my life, whenever things began to hurt so badly that my only emotions were frustration and depression, somehow, a support system was available when I needed it. All of these groups had a few things in common: mothers brought together through their children, friends of friends gathering through mutual acquaintances, all of us sharing information, concern, and ourselves."

At times, however, in our daily involvement with our natural support groups, we lose sight of the ways in which we give and receive support. We get bogged down in problems, routine, and unthinking responses. When this happens some of us may feel the need to seek a renewed sense of support in outside, or intentional, support groups, in which we can re-evaluate with some objectivity what our natural support structures offer us and what we can contribute to them. While a feeling of support can and usually does grow within these intentional groups, their real purpose is to redirect our recognition and affirmation back to our primary sources of support—ourselves and the people who are part of our everyday life.

Parent support groups have a special purpose. Within them we are encouraged to explore and define our attitudes about childhood and parenting. By examining child-nurturing philosophies and weighing them against personal experiences, value systems, and the concepts of affirmation, people deepen their understanding of their own style of parenting and gain insight into the parenting styles of others. A parent support group, therefore, is not a therapy group, a social gathering, a debating society, or a place to find "the way." It provides a forum for appreciating parents and children and a chance to be enriched by the company of others with a common interest and concern—parenting. It offers a resource bank of information, skills, ideas, and assistance. It is a working place in which individuals are encouraged to strengthen their parenting insights and skills. Most of all, a parent support group gives parents the opportunity to find affirmation of the special qualities and strengths that each person brings to parenting.

One woman who helped organize a parent support group described her experience this way:

"Our group grew out of a need among diverse women in an urban setting to share experiences and problem-solving ideas. Observing the extent of the isolation and the random nature of contacts among friends and neighbors, we brought the group together in our capacity as facilitators-participants. As group members, we were affected by the urban setting, with its emphasis on self-sufficiency and social privacy; we wanted to become more involved with our friends and neighbors who were under similar pressure.

"Thus began our experience of formalizing the process of sharing into a group meeting. In general, we observed a strengthening of

THE ART OF GIVING AND RECEIVING SUPPORT

self-confidence, as group members developed a sense of their common situations and of the affirmation of being needed by each other. The support received was evident in various ways, not the least of which was the emphasis on listening. Learning that it was possible and permissible to talk about feelings and problems, and that everyone had them, was an important development. Not only did we realize that vulnerability was a widespread, acceptable quality, but also that 'problems' were no longer a stigma and could be accepted as a normal fact of being vital, individual human beings.

"The group *per se* did not last many meetings for logistical reasons, but the caring and sense of unity were there and continued to develop so that when the meetings themselves ceased, we still felt that the group had served its purpose. Various members continued to maintain relationships with each other, sharing joys and problems, going out together, and generally benefiting from having had encounters at a deeper level."

Sometimes there is one common goal or problem that draws a group of parents together. In recent years we have seen growing numbers of parents band together to support each other in confronting special problems, such as parents of children with physical or emotional disabilities, or parents of children with drug or alcohol problems. In some cases groups center around problems that the parents themselves have in common: single parenting, for instance. Regardless of the special need or motivation of the group, the goal should always be the same: the affirmation and strengthening of the members as nurtured and nurturing individuals.

3 When my parents and I moved from my grandmother's home to our own in another community, I quickly established relationships with older neighbors to replace those I'd lost with my relatives. An elderly couple, Gramps and Aunt Gertie, were "adopted." Gramps had a woodworking shop, where he made birdhouses, weather vanes, tables, and all manner of wind-driven lawn ornaments. I stood for hours watching him at work, and as I grew older he encouraged me to paint or hammer on his projects. Eventually he oversaw my original wood creations. Not only was the experience of learning the proper use and care of tools an invaluable nonsexist lesson for a young girl in the fifties, but a genuine feeling of self-respect grew as I explored and experienced pride in my abilities. A shar-

When Generations Come Together

ing evolved that was rooted in that respect. Hours passed quickly as Gramps spoke of his past or I told of escapades at school. We shared meals, thousands of wintergreen Life Savers, and cool, dusky evenings of rocking on the porch. As our family grew, Gramps and Aunt Gertie's home became a peaceful haven for me (and also, I have since learned, for my mother!). They listened to and encouraged my curiosity, and affirmed my capabilities. I see now that my dependence upon their perspective and concern satisfied their desire to be needed: They felt valued for the abilities they possessed.

Such intergenerational relationships were common to the extended families of the past but are rare in our transient, age-graded society. As businesses sort and shuffle employees across continents, many families resign themselves to separation and the loss of intimacy across generations; even when families remain geographically close, this age-based separation occurs. Our society has come to define and group us chronologically. From childhood on we are thrust into institutionalized age groups: play groups, kindergartens, elementary schools, scouts, colleges, young

This chapter was written by Penni Eldredge-Martin.

marrieds, parents of teens, nursing homes, senior citizens' clubs. Often deliberately, sometimes unwittingly, we expect, encourage, and participate primarily in relationships with those of like ages; and in *Catch Twenty-Two* fashion, this intergenerational inexperience further distances children and parents.

One grandmother worried about her eleven-year-old granddaughter's impending visit: "But I don't even know her! What can we talk about? We don't have anything in common." Yet, both have a deep love of nature, each one gardens, finding solace in the warm earth, and the younger one expresses her feelings in poetry. Though they have much in common, they do not share it. Since each seldom interacts outside her age group, their visits together are marked by painful silences and awkward, disjointed attempts at conversation. Sadly, each one misses not only meaningful sharing, but also the unique understanding and support that can flourish when deeply felt needs are identified.

Isolation exacts its costs. By not developing the ability to relate and engender trust across generations, we lose many opportunities for sharing and learning a broader range of communicative skills, insights, and responsibilities; we forfeit many of the accumulated, imaginative human resources available to us, and, most important, we are denied some tangible sources of hope and support that can be gained from these shared perspectives.

The changing definition of family adds to the confusion and frustration of parents and children in search of a strong support base. The currently revived concept of the "traditional" American family (remember Dick, Jane, Sally, and Spot?) ignores the statistic that by 1984 more than half the children entering first grade in this country will be from single-parent homes.[1] When the nuclear-family stereotype is heralded by politicians, religious leaders, and others, and the reality ignored, parents and children feel invalidated, flawed, and guilty for not measuring up to the perfect image. Supermoms

---

[1] Willis B. Goldbeck, Executive Director of the Washington Business Group on Health, Washington, D.C., quoted at the Women in Crisis Conference, held in New York City, June 30, 1981.

WHEN GENERATIONS COME TOGETHER

and superdads struggle to fill the gap and meet the demands of home, family, and career, while their personal needs often go unmet. Children in single-parent families are often influenced by reading materials and class discussions in which the family is represented as including Mom, Dad, brothers, and/or sisters; it is no wonder that they question how they are categorized, living alone with only one parent. Expanded intergenerational relationships can ease these pressures by extending nurturing supportive commitments and resources beyond our immediate families and our individual age groups. As we actively build more diversified sources of support, we receive important affirmation by experiencing equality, responsibility, and power outside our traditional roles. Regardless of age, we all seek and grow from such validation, and enrich our families with new perceptions and appreciation of ourselves and our abilities.

Ageism

Bridges between generations are not easily built. We all perpetuate, consciously and unconsciously, age-based assumptions about others that blind us to their abilities and impede their, and our, personal growth. One of the first questions asked of a child is, "How old are you?" as though by assigning a number his likes, dislikes, needs, capabilities, and limits will all become clear. Of those past twenty, the question may not be openly asked, but similar assessments and assumptions still are often made: people over ninety are senile; around forty, one enters a midlife crisis; adolescents must rebel, two-year-olds are terrors to live with. This ageist thinking leads us to respond to stereotypes rather than to unique individuals, and our expectations may unwittingly orchestrate the "realities."

Perhaps the most insidious and pervasive age-related assumptions are those made about the appropriate assignment of responsibility. From a myriad of ageist generalizations we have arrived at a social system that implies that the capacity for responsible behavior appears and disappears magically at certain chronological intervals. Society dictates that the major portion of responsibility belongs to adults of middle years. Designated as the primary caretakers of the young, the elderly, and in many cases the disabled, there is an expectation that they are, by virtue of their years, naturally imbued with sensitivity, strength, capability, farsightedness, and unerring fairness. Children, though encouraged to practice responsibility, are considered too immature to own it. On the other hand, senior citizens, considered our models of maturity, are systematically "relieved" of responsibility, as if they traded in their strength, wisdom, and mental acuity when they became eligible for pension or Medicare. Each of us, to varying degrees, is both the victim and the perpetrator of an ageist society. Through re-evaluation of our age-based assumptions we can uncover and encourage greater human resources.

In an intergenerational workshop Peter, six, and Sherry, thirty-five, were paired in a Trust Walk.[2] This exercise calls for two partners to take turns being blindfolded and guided around the neighborhood by the "sighted" partner. While Sherry was blindfolded she suddenly realized that Peter was leading her toward a busy intersection without traffic signals. Later, when she and Peter shared their experience with the group, Sherry confessed:

"My first impulse was to stop and say, 'Remember, we must look both ways.' I remembered the ground rule to trust my partner, and forced myself not to say anything; but I got more and more nervous as we approached the curb. Suddenly Peter stopped and said to me, 'Now I'll look both ways before we cross.' "

When Sherry reached this point in her description, Peter interjected: "I knew it all along! You just worried about it sooner than I did!"

By becoming alert to opportunities for letting go, by checking our own responses and allowing others to be responsible for making choices, we can cut the bonds of age stereotyping and encourage

---

[2] Robert C. Hawley and Isabel L. Hawley, "Observation Walk," in *Developing Human Potential: A Handbook of Activities for Personal and Social Growth* (Amherst, Mass.: ERA Press, 1975), p. 44. See also p. 156.

new growth. True responsibility can and must be learned through tangible decision-making experiences that include obligations to any results.

The contract system used in many open classrooms provides children with experience in "owning" and practicing responsibility. Lynn, Joy, and Amy were summer day-care teachers in such a classroom for five-year-olds. Each Monday they met with the children. As each child completed a plan for the week's activities, it was recorded on a large sheet of paper and posted. Both individual and group activities then followed from these plans, and each child was involved in the preparations. Early in the summer, not only were the children unaccustomed to such responsibility, but their responses showed that they were unskilled in thinking and planning ahead. Unsure as to whether their plans could be used as guides, the children relied upon the usual choices: swim trips, playing outside, and drawing; but as practice and trust evolved, the planning process became a source of excitement and pride, an opportunity to make real choices about their own education. Toward summer's end the children decided that, as a group, they wanted to learn to read.

Sherry and Peter had firsthand insights into accountability and equality. Students in Amy, Joy and Lynn's classroom learned to trust themselves as well as the adults who respected their right and ability to make meaningful plans. The perceptions gained by these intergenerational exchanges can lead to important first steps in upending ageist attitudes and experiencing supportive, alternative relationships.

Intentional intergenerational relationships provide opportunities that allow us to reverse stereotypes, to explore our needs and our strengths, to learn skills that develop our listening and sensitivity, and to become aware of the responsibility that accompanies asking for and giving support. Nurturing such commitments affirms us and others in the belief that each of us, regardless of age, is a source of valuable information, understanding, and ability. In the family setting, personal insights and resources ease parent-child pressures and make way for new possibilities.

Equality and Power

While I was sitting cross-legged on the floor at a parent-support-group meeting, a ten-month-old crawled around me for five minutes. He inspected me from various angles, touching my sneakers and pants cuffs. I extended a finger and wiggled it in the air. First he followed it with his eyes, then reached out to grab it. Finally he pulled himself up on his mother's shoulder and lunged into my lap, where he sat contentedly for the next fifteen minutes.

There was a time when I would have reached for the child the moment he was within an arm's length, probably setting off a disruptive scene of panicky and tearful retreat. Instead, when this child's actions signaled an interest, my extended finger indicated a similar curiosity: "Yes, you're pretty interesting, too!" Even after he grabbed my finger, I waited for him to decide. By respectfully matching my response to his inquiry, remaining open and welcoming, and by not making any assumptions, we approached each other on equal terms.

Power over others is demonstrated in many subtle ways. Just the necessity to look up or down at another person can establish a physical sense of inequality. The ten-month-old felt free to examine my sneakers and pants cuffs because I sat on the floor at his height. Had I stood or sat in a chair, the likelihood of our interacting would have diminished. The typical adult response—picking up the child —though intended to encourage or engage, would instead have emphasized my physical strength and power. The relationship would have felt unequal to the child. This is not to say that adults should be standoffish; gestures of invitation and openness—wiggling a finger or quietly sitting near the child for example—respectfully allow acceptance or rejection; and permit the child, because the decision is his, to feel and be powerful. Physical and emotional closeness to others, the feeling of comfort and of being accepted and loved, is an important source of support; but we need to be particularly aware and respectful of the signals sent by others, especially by children and the elderly. Indications of readiness or willingness to interact are each person's right; assumptions are inappropriate. Friendliness and warmth differ from solicitousness; we must learn to wait patiently for an opening and if it occurs, follow up.

When responsibility for dependent children and others is interpreted in terms of power *over* them, it may result in denying people the right to make decisions and to feel powerful or validated. It becomes a barrier to positive relationships and mutually productive exchanges. Just as power can be used to include, it can also be used to exclude. Carrie, an outgoing, young-at-heart, eighty-five-year-old widow, was proud of her independence. She sought out a diversified group of friends to keep her life interesting. She joined civic groups and little theater, participated in "family fun" nights at her church, attended school concerts and programs in her neighborhood, and responded eagerly to invitations to visit classrooms to show slides and talk about her time in the Peace Corps in Africa at age seventy. When she was suddenly hospitalized for minor surgery, staff doctors and social workers noted her undeniable forgetfulness, lumped it together with her Bohemian life style and her opinionated and at times irascible way of talking, and declared her senile—incompetent of caring for herself. Within a week her power of attorney was usurped, her clothing and furniture packed off to the local rescue mission, and she was delivered by ambulance to a nursing home miles away from her community. Ageist assumptions and the use of power to control, terminated the mutually beneficial interaction between Carrie and her community.

Sharing responsibility and power across generational barriers generates supportive new resources for groups and individuals, families, schools, and communities. Young people have many sensitive, creative abilities and fresh insights to share with those younger and older. The elderly possess a wealth of skills quickly being lost in our technological society, and are springs of wisdom and warmth as well. Reciprocal, affirmative relationships can make available to all the experiences of power, equality, and responsibility; such realization can be a deep source of hope and comfort in a stressed world.

Many families accept and perpetuate the myth that their members

can and should be all things to one another, regardless of circumstances. Often adults will need to demonstrate to children—sometimes verbally, but even more effectively through role modeling—the fact that meaningful support relationships can be found outside one's immediate family. It's important that families come to appreciate and accept that each member may define and establish her own personal support system. When an individual avails himself of this right, he should be viewed as capable and resourceful, not as a threat; and other family members needn't feel guilty because they could not fulfill his needs.

At a week-long religious conference at a college campus, a special rapport developed between six-year-old David and forty-year-old Karen. One day he asked her to have lunch with him, and from that invitation a series of luncheon and dinner "engagements" occurred at the cafeteria. David and Karen each sought and found a warm, emotional bond with someone outside their age group. David's father knew of Karen and was confident that David was in good company. He did not impose himself on the relationship; he respected and welcomed the friendship that grew between his son and another adult. David was learning to develop his own sources of input and support, and David, his father, and Karen all benefited.

The reciprocity of intergenerational relationships rests upon heightened sensitivity to another's needs. By recognizing and, if possible, meeting such needs, each person feels worthwhile. At ninety, Bill was a man whose former physical prowess was steadily ebbing away. Still, he doggedly sought meaningful things to do. Recognizing his father's intense desire to feel and be productive, and overworked in his own job, Brooks brought his infant son's bookcase and highchair to be refinished. The final products were a source of pride for Bill, particularly because they were real contributions that met both his son's and grandson's needs. For an important moment, the generational scale was in balance.

All personal relationships flourish when the commonalities that are shared are recognized and appreciated. David and Karen delighted in games, imaginative stories, and laughter. Brooks and his father shared a love of wood and of "having a project to do." With these mutual interests as a starting point, each experienced intergenerational sharing and growing, in which sensitivity and listening were paramount. The insights, dialogue, and trust engendered by such awareness meant that any future differences or conflicts would be weighed against what they had shared together. The distance between them had been lessened. When people feel capable of finding resources that will support and improve their lives, they are more willing to risk new ideas and accept challenges. Their imagination and energy powerfully charge our families' and communities' emotional batteries. Ageism, on the other hand, drains us all. Our loss of contact across generations can leave us feeling overburdened and incompetent. What we need is not only the confidence but the context in which to highlight, enhance, and use our abilities.

Elise Boulding, a sociologist at Dartmouth College, holds that much essential family nurturing is, and has always been, done by children, but that adults do not recognize or value it as such.[3] Caring

---

[3] See also the Annotated Bibliography, p. 173.

for and attending to others should not be a task reserved solely for parents, teachers, or nursing staff. Children have deep reserves of strength, creativity, and perception, and love to share with the adult world. But again, we must be open to their awareness and acknowledge its presence. One evening my husband was late for dinner, a casserole was drying out in the oven, the sewing project had failed, and my fifteen-month-old son had reached his "hungry and haranguing hour." Worried and depressed, I suddenly crouched in the dining room, sobbing. Andrew stood quietly watching me for a few moments, then turned and walked into the living room. He returned with his "bee-bee," his favorite blanket, outstretched to me. Yes, his gesture helped me, I told him. After a few hugs, we proceeded to finish preparations for dinner. Reaching beyond himself and his needs, he shared with me what he knew of comfort; his simple gesture and my acknowledgment of it said we were equal at that moment. It was a moving, powerful experience for each of us.

Where Do We Find and How Do We Nurture Intergenerational Relationships?

Since relationships over wide age ranges are not currently the norm, finding them requires a commitment: a willingness to challenge ageist assumptions about children, the elderly, and ourselves. In a way, we are breaking new ground or trying to reclaim land that has lain fallow. We must unearth and examine the conscious and unconscious stereotypes that have grown up, the effortless categories assigned by virtue of age. We must overcome our inexperience by taking risks and by divesting ourselves of some of the overwhelming responsibilities and powers bestowed upon us, so that we may know experientially the support and nurturance to be found in reciprocal, intergenerational relationships.

Your life may hold many opportunities for such interactions. If so, you are lucky. Most, however, will need to make concerted efforts toward such relationships, investing time and energy in seeking out and nurturing them. Some parents recognize and encourage other adults to share particular interests with their children, as in the case of a single father who boards two male college students. Hans appreciates the friendship between these young men and his eleven-year-old son and twelve-year-old daughter: "They enjoy more of the children's sports and outdoor recreational interests and abilities than I do, and the children love their interest."

Other families invite people of differing age groups to partake in special family activities. At Christmas the Carters, Nancy and Dan and one-year-old Drew, asked four junior-high-school friends to join them in cutting down and making decorations for their first Christmas tree. The cold, blustery day was warmed with laughter, stories, charades, originality, carol singing, and pizza making and eating. In much the same way, Nancy and Dan had developed a caring relationship with a seventy-year-old neighbor. Albert lived alone and was often seen walking briskly into a nearby wood. Avid bird watchers and wildflower enthusiasts, Nancy and Dan sensed a kindred spirit. Their questions about native birds were rewarded by a wealth of excited, detailed information, shared over simple meals and during keen-sighted forays into the woods.

Various structured programs have been designed to promote intergenerational relationships. Some communities have realized that important sources of skills, local history, and warm emotion lie dormant and untapped within senior-citizen complexes and nursing homes. One response, in the Ann Arbor, Michigan, school system, has been the development of Teaching-Learning Communities,[4] a program bringing senior citizens into classrooms as skill sharers and as teachers' aides. The emphasis is not wholly on the concrete, however, for as skills sharpen, vital human connections are made. The widespread perspectives and deepened insights shared across desks and generations are palpable experiences in the continuity of human feelings, events, and abilities. Around the country, programs are springing up that encourage the participation of older community members. Many schools now have grandparent days and en-

---

[4] Ann Arbor Public Schools, *Teaching-Learning Communities* (Ann Arbor, Mich.: Carol H. Tice, 1972).

courage the participation of grandparents and other elderly persons in the classrooms and on field trips. Many housing complexes and suburban communities have started programs—one in New York is called Generations Working Together—to encourage fun, mutual assistance, and sharing across the generation gap.

Friends Center, a complex housing a number of Quaker and other organizations in downtown Philadelphia, has established a day-care facility for employees' children, from infants to three years. Its addition to the center has had many positive results: watching children at play in the courtyard gives a boost to weary workers, parents are close by if illness or accidents occur, and parents' work and commuting experience takes on a tangible form for the children. In addition the children and all of the adults at the complex have begun to form relationships with people of different age groups, beyond their own families. All adults in the complex are encouraged to have lunch, visit, and read to the children whenever possible. Many special friendships have blossomed in this setting; adults and children, both, return to their work and their homes with new perceptions and sensitivities.

The Unitarian Church of Santa Barbara, California, sought a deepened sense of affinity within its spiritual community. Groups of fourteen to sixteen diverse volunteers—whole families, singles, parents without partners, teens—were organized into "family clusters," contracting to meet twice a month for an initial three-month period. Each cluster developed its own particular concept of meaningful interaction, with the help of a facilitator whose role was to act as a resource person for as short as time as possible, and then become an equal member of the group. This latter requirement stressed group members' equal responsibility for the group itself, and allowed the facilitator to experience his own role within the community:

> They help each other with work that needs doing around the homes of members: painting, lot clearing, repairs, and the like. One member bought a new home recently, and since it needed some painting and plumbing, the whole family stepped in to help, did so with pleasure. It drew them closer together still.

One family met at the beach for breakfast at sunrise, and many family members go to lunch together after church. One family spent a weekend at the beach house of a member, another spent a weekend at a cottage at Mammoth Lake, another still went off to Mexico for a time. Campouts are common; so are social evenings. Members often meet together in twos, threes and fours, as well as at the gatherings of the whole family. They keep in touch by phone. Some have taken shut-in people into their circle of concern. The activity patterns, in short, are rich and quite various, many of them generated spontaneously.

It is not yet clear what the families will eventually become: Each is autonomous, will create its own, unique form, determine its own destiny, on its own initiative, at its own pace. Whatever they ultimately become, their present existence has already justified the thought, discussion, labor and anxiety that went into their creation.[5]

Confronting ageist stereotypes, experiencing equality, and sharing power and support beyond our family and our peer group are concerns so new to us that they may seem burdensome and unwieldy. For this reason, controlled settings—such as those in Ann Arbor and Santa Barbara—in which to discuss perceptions and practice skills may be helpful. Another approach is an intergenerational workshop or seminar, at which carefully structured, firsthand, cross-generational activities may lead to discussions and insights based upon personal experiences. In these settings, participants, hearing of others' past and present struggles with feelings and needs, angers, joys, and uncertainties, can experience affirmation and support as their commonalities unfold across the generations.

Two Friends Meetings in Germantown, Pennsylvania, traditionally gather their families together in the autumn for an evening of fellowship; they enjoy a potluck supper, and the apple desserts celebrate the young people's apple harvest of the previous weekend. One year they decided that this intergenerational tradition should have a

---

[5] Unitarian Church of Santa Barbara, *Developing an Extended Family Program* (Santa Barbara: Unitarian Church of Santa Barbara, undated report), p. 9. For additional information write 1535 Santa Barbara Street, Santa Barbara, Calif., 93109.

more specific focus. In the past, adults had gathered in one place and children in another, or families had stayed together; this time they sought deepened community, through sharing across age and family groupings. With the help of two facilitators, Meeting members planned an hour-and-a-half-long gathering. The harvesters composed "apple carols" (the traditional Christmas carol "Deck the Halls" became, "Deck the halls with apple peelings, Gather here to share our feelings, Share apple gifts from Earth our Mother, Think of peace and of each other, *Fa-la-la-la-la, la-la-la-la*"), and the lyrics were posted so the evening could begin with singing. After a get-acquainted name game, in which participants lined up in "apple-betical" order, the facilitators led the group through an increasingly interactive program of games and exercises. They bobbed for, peeled, and balanced apples, and in small groups were drawn into safe, lighthearted conversation, telling tall tales about their apples and making up group stories to share with the larger gathering. To close the evening, everyone held hands in a large circle, and each affirmed a meaningful part of the evening.[6]

Intergenerational workshops have been designed for groups ranging in size from twelve to three hundred, and the length of programs has also varied: one hour, a weekend, daily two-hour sessions over a week's time. All have four major goals in common:

1. to have fun, to celebrate and affirm our joy in life and in living.
2. to develop better communication skills between people of differing ages.
3. to recognize and name the resources and skills of those present.
4. to enable and encourage participants, through the experience of the workshop, to pursue intergenerational relationships in their own lives.

This last goal is paramount. As with affirmation, some individuals may need safe, controlled settings, such as workshops (or extended-family programs or teaching-learning communities), in which to

---

[6] For additional information on structuring an intergenerational workshop, see p. 146.

practice skills and experience the benefits of moving beyond and then returning to the family and familiar age group; workshops, however, cannot replace the experience of an authentic intergenerational relationship.

By whatever method we come together outside and within our families or age groups, relationships ultimately must grow between individuals, and must be respected as their sole responsibility. As parents become the models for the acceptability of intimate intergenerational, nonfamilial relationships, they must be careful to respect and sensitively accept similar gestures on the part of the children. The right to extend one's family can and should be the responsibility of all its members. Overcoming the biases of ageism and inexperience by risking ourselves in authentic intergenerational relationships may be difficult, but the rewards, the moments of magic, are too great not to try. And as individuals whose strength

and joy is derived from deep commitments to our families, shouldn't we seek all the resources available to nurture them?

As our competencies and repertoires expand through intergenerational relationships and return ultimately to enrich our families, we see and experience the vastness of our human resources as revealed in each one of us—our creativity, our imagination, our energy, our skills, our capacity for joy and intimacy, our resiliency, our commitment. Freed to acknowledge and trust these assets, we are affirmed and supported as powerful individuals, essential, valued members of strong and resilient families. From this knowing springs hope.

4 Affirmative communication—the accurate and affirming sending and receiving of information—is essential to developing and maintaining nurturing relationships. Communication is inevitable. Even if we sit motionless, blank-faced, without saying a word, we are sending a message: "I won't!" "I can't!" or "I mustn't!" Since we cannot avoid communicating, we must be sure that our messages accurately represent us; we must learn to interpret messages correctly so that we can respond to them appropriately. Through words, facial expressions, touches, posture, we offer (or withhold) our thoughts and feelings for consideration and invite (or exclude) the views and insights of others. Accurately communicating our thoughts and feelings allows us to share our ideas and dreams with others and

Talking It Over— Not Taking It Out

to get feedback on our perceptions. If we communicate accurately, we can make known our needs and define or request the necessary support to get those needs met. When accurate communications are based in affirmation—in an attitude of respect, appreciation, and positive expectation—they encourage new understanding and growth. At the heart of affirmative communication is the belief that each person is special *because* of his age, sex, diverse background, experience, and unique personality, and is therefore a valuable source of information. Through the clear, honest, and open sharing of that information, the giver, the receiver and their community are enriched.

Being open is basic to affirmative communication. The honest and free-flowing exchange of ideas and feelings is an invitation to reciprocal sharing, to testing and expanding our concepts jointly and discovering common ground for mutual assistance and support. It asserts that each of us has something to learn and something worth sharing. Openness in communication often feels risky and requires self-confidence and trust in others. It's a two-way proposition. When we say exactly what we think and feel, we make ourselves vulnerable; when someone communicates openly with us, it usually places on us a feeling of obligation to match that open-ness, and a sense of responsibility as well. Being open to straight-forward exchanges of information challenges us to reaffirm or reconsider our point of view, perhaps to re-evaluate fundamental truths that mold our values and life styles. In open communication issues cannot be ducked. Information is candidly exchanged in an open and affirming way. We say and hear things we like and agree with, as well as those we don't like and disagree with. In return for our risk-taking we gain opportunities to give and receive informa-tion that could be put to effective use. When open communication is based in affirmation, it does not involve confronting, accusing, or dumping feelings on someone. Instead it entails sharing honestly, with an expectation that information communicated affirmingly will be acted on positively and appropriately.

Systems of Communication

Language itself can become a barrier to understanding and being understood. Jargon and slang, fancy words, facial expressions and body language, rather than facilitating it, often get in the way of communicating. A cold stare, a hands-on-hips or arms-crossed-over-the-chest pose can shut down a conversation without a word. Using "in" talk sets up exclusive groups that prevent both the insid-ers and the outsiders from gaining new perspectives and potentially useful counsel. By developing a broad vocabulary of clear, varied, and inclusive verbal, facial, and body expressions, we make greater understanding possible through affirming communication.

The value of a creative and flexible language became clear to me when I visited my husband's family in Germany. I knew only enough conversational German to cover my basic needs and to exchange polite amenities. To make sense of the reunion, to contribute and feel included, I had to watch and listen intently for every nuance, every discernible syllable. Fred's family, sympathetic to my struggle, directed their comments to me, talking slower, using facial expres-sions, gestures, touches, and choices of words. Patiently Fred translated my responses to them into German, and a deeper level of understanding grew between us as he focused on conveying not just my words but my feelings. By working together creatively, we were able to create a language we could all share. Though communications in our normal relationships do not usually require this much effort, they certainly do deserve this much sensitivity, creativity, and interest.

Because what each of us has to communicate is unique, expecting clairvoyance, no matter how well we feel we know people, can lead to muddled communications and relationships. Kathy and Joan, two teen-age school friends, had worked all summer preparing for the cheerleading tryouts at school. In the final round of tryouts Kathy was eliminated, but Joan was selected for the team. That night Joan called Kathy for a French assignment, but neither girl mentioned cheerleading. The next day Kathy ignored Joan and refused her offer of a ride home, with an icy glare: "Don't do me any favors! You don't care about me, anyway!" Kathy snarled.

"But you know I do!" Joan stammered.

"Oh, sure, that's why you never said a word about my not making the team, even though you knew how much I needed to talk about it."

"No, Kathy!" Joan gasped. "When you didn't bring it up, I thought you didn't want to talk about it. I didn't want to upset you!"

Kathy, fighting back tears, choked, "We've been friends since sixth grade. You *had* to know how I felt!"

We affirm the specialness of our feelings and ideas when we recognize that while other people can understand and care about them, no one else can define and express them as truly as we can.

Affirmation as the Basic Message

Situations and circumstances have an enormous effect on the manner in which we communicate, but with affirmation as the base, the tone of all communications can impart a sense of trust and mutual good will. Affirming communication expects and encourages people to draw on their best resources and most cooperative instincts. When we must assume an authoritative posture we need to be especially careful to communicate in a positive way, without threats or insults, but also without being demeaning or patronizing.

There are times when each one of us must make decisions, take action, and secure the cooperation of others by giving information in a firm but reasonable manner: "Come out of the street, *now!*" or "Mom, quick! The sink is overflowing!" The directions can be given in a manner that indicates: This is what is needed from you now. I believe that you can and will do it.

When it is necessary to set limits we can affirm the other person by acknowledging and respecting her feelings, but making it clear when, by whom, or in what way certain behavior is not acceptable: "Barbie, I understand that you are feeling bored and frustrated about waiting for the doctor to see you, but you cannot run and be noisy in the waiting room. Some other people here are not feeling well." In setting affirming limits we must never reject or disqualify the other person's feelings: "Barbie, you haven't been here long enough to be bored!" nor should we use manipulation, teasing, or sarcasm to get cooperation. If a diversion seems appropriate, it is stated explicitly: "Let's find a magazine with pretty pictures in it, and we can sit quietly and talk about them." In setting limits affirmingly we must state respectfully but firmly what can or cannot be tolerated: "Mom, I am really tired tonight, I'm not up to talking about my grades. I'd like to talk with you about it in the morning."

When we give information to increase understanding or clarify issues, we can do so without implying superiority. We may need to supply pragmatic information such as telling a teen-ager what it will cost for him to be included in the family's car-insurance policy; or we may want to share about our feelings on an issue: "When you're late, I think that the car might have broken down or that there has been an accident. I feel anxious," but we can affirm the other person by supplying only the information that is relevant and helpful, without lecturing or moralizing about it.

When we ask questions to further our own understanding of a situation, we must take care not to probe or invade the other's privacy, and never attempt to trap others with questions to which we already have (or think we have) the answer: "Joe, who do you suppose left this popsicle stick on the sofa?" Instead we pose respectful questions that will bring new light to a situation and will help us be more positive contributors to the relationship.

Each of us is an authority on our own reactions to the behavior of people close to us. It can be helpful (and sometimes surprising) to learn how we seem to others, but when sharing these insights we should present our perceptions noncritically without shaming or providing our analysis of the behavior: "You know, when Jane and Benji have friends here to play, you tease them a lot"; not, "You act bratty when the other kids have friends over! You are jealous and insecure!" Offering insights rather than judgments allows people to take responsibility for their own behavior, to draw conclusions, provide additional input, and, if necessary, work on making changes.

Sometimes our exchanges must take the form of negotiation. In affirming communications each person shares equally in the role of negotiator. Both must define the problem briefly from their point of view, list their needs, and work together to determine what each can give and is willing to accept.[1] Negotiation is a process that demands mutual respect and equal involvement. It should not be used to maneuver or bargain a person into an agreement. The goal is compromise without force. In relationships in which communications are positive and effective, most interactions should be worked out before a feeling of stalemate arises, thus avoiding the need for negotiation. This method of communication requires too much energy to be going on most of the time; but, when necessary, affirming communicators can negotiate resolutions because they operate from a base of trust and affirmation.

Listening

Careful listening facilitates open communications. When we risk the open honest sharing of our thoughts and feelings, we need and

---

[1] For a complete description of this process, see Setting Positive Limits, p. 97.

deserve to be fully heard. An attentive listener provides safety and encouragement for genuine sharing. The first step is to create a positive listening environment by clearing away distractions and giving the speaker our full attention. It isn't always necessary or desirable to bring all activity to a dead stop. Low-involvement activities, such as sharing a cup of coffee or a snack, folding wash, or taking a walk together, are often good backdrops for light, thoughtful discussion. Crises or issues of great urgency or emotion require an atmosphere of undiluted consideration. Care should be given to providing a special time and setting that is physically comfortable and private. The primary requirement, however, is a listener's attentive and receptive mind and spirit. If you've just walked in the door and are rain-soaked and headachey when someone arrives with an urgent need to be listened to, the most conscientious response is to insist, firmly but lovingly, on the time necessary to first pull yourself together; if need be, to state truthfully your present unsuitability as a listener. This designates you as a caring listener and the other person as deserving of undivided attention.

The listener's job is to convey interest and to demonstrate an attitude of support. The sharer needs to know that the listener is really hearing and is open to what is being said. The listener could, for example, sit close to the sharer, accept eye contact freely, relax her own body, and offer quiet acknowledgments, such as nodding, touching, or just a few simple words: "Go on" or "What else?" Responses need to be short, nonjudgmental, matched in tone and intensity to what is being said, and directed toward easing the job of the sharer.[2]

An involved listener might ask questions occasionally to clarify his understanding of the problem, but these questions should never be probing or leading. From time to time the listener restates his understanding of what has been said. If it is incorrect, it can be re-explained; if it is accurate, the speaker is reassured that her message is being clearly understood. Placating or soothing can

---

[2] For more on listening, see also Thomas Gordon's *P.E.T. in Action*, especially pp. 46–50 (see the Annotated Bibliography, p. 174).

TALKING IT OVER—NOT TAKING IT OUT

short-circuit communications. An "It's not really that bad!" reply implies faulty judgment on the part of the sharer. The listener must be aware that what is being said is an accurate description of what the sharer feels at the time. It is real and deserves acknowledgement.

An important part of listening is noting and appreciating the steps taken and the progress made by the sharer: "You've thought a lot about this," or, "You've already tried plan A and plan B." We often fail to credit ourselves for our good efforts, and it is encouraging to hear them noted by others.

A caring listener never steals the show by drawing conclusions or giving unsolicited advice. To do so is a negation of the other person's ability as a problem solver. An affirming listener, a partner in effective communication, will assist the sharer in reaching her own best answers: "What do you think could happen?" "How might you do that?" The listener demonstrates his involvement without taking the primary action away from the person who is seeking to be heard.

Listening is the side of effective communication for which most of us have had little training. The following group listening exercise is a mechanism for observing and getting feedback about one's listening skills. Divide the group into working groups of three (or four, if necessary). In the small groups designate the roles of sharer, listener, and observer (in groups of four, there will be two observers). The sharer speaks for three minutes about an assigned topic, such as, "If I could give a televised speech about anything I wanted, it would be about . . . because. . . ." While the sharer speaks, the listener gives his full attention: acknowledging, accepting, and, when necessary, clarifying what he has heard, all without distracting the sharer in any way. The observers focus their attention on the listener. After three minutes, the listener summarizes what he has heard and allows the sharer to indicate whether her message has been correctly received. The observers then give feedback to the listener; they first affirm his special listening strengths, then indicate any specific barriers to his receiving information accurately. The roles are then rotated. After each member of the small group has had an opportunity to be both the listener and the sharer, the large group assembles to discuss not only what members found difficult about being an attentive listener but also how it felt as a sharer to have an attentive listener available.[3]

Feedback

Giving and getting feedback affirmingly is an important part of effective communication. Positive feedback that encourages rather than criticizes is given in an open-ended, nonbinding way. Being invited to give someone feedback—"What do you think?" "What should I do?"—does not entitle or qualify us to specify or expect change. It is essential to give input without judgments or demands attached: Instead of stating, "You are wrong, you must do it like this," we can offer encouragement: "If I had to deal with this, I would rather do it this way. . . ." People must find their own best approaches to problems, based on their values and life experiences.

I-Messages,[4] a communication tool outlined by Dr. Thomas Gordon in his book *P.E.T. in Action*, are especially useful in giving feedback about personal behavior in an affirming way. The I-Message gives information without placing blame or taking charge of the

---

[3] For more about expressing and re-evaluating feelings, read Harvey Jackins, *The Human Side of Human Beings*. See the Annotated Bibliography, p. 175.

[4] See the Annotated Bibliography, p. 174.

other person's problem. It indicates confidence in the individual's ability to act caringly and responsibly in addressing his own problematic behavior. I-Messages state the behavior that is in question, the feelings that it evokes, and the tangible effect that it has on the other person: "When you whine about what you want, I feel frustrated, because I can't understand what you are saying." Feedback given in this way allows the judgment to be made by the owner of the behavior. It does not give answers or solutions, though it is specific enough to suggest areas to consider.

When we receive feedback about our behavior, we must affirm ourselves and the giver by accepting it—positive or negative—as valuable data presented to us by someone who has experienced how we come across to him. Sometimes the more astute the feedback, the more difficult it is to accept and assimilate. As the old adage goes: The truth hurts. At times we are tempted to seek feedback only from people who will tell us what we want to hear. If we are feeling down and need some guaranteed affirmation, it may be a good idea to seek out a reliable fan for an ego boost; but if doubts or problems remain, we will need to affirm ourselves enough to seek some straight talk—objective feedback—about what others feel we could be doing better or differently, as well as what they feel we are already doing well. In doing so we recognize and exhibit our personal strength, our faith in relationships, and our desire to grow.

Distress created by feedback may in itself give us useful information. It may signal fear, remorse, anger, relief: "I must do this, but it is scary," "I have been wrong," "I hate hearing this!" or "I can do nothing more." The responsibility of accepting or not accepting, sorting out, and working through feedback belongs to the receiver. The feelings about the feedback belong to her and are legitimate. The person offering the feedback affirms the receiver by accepting whatever reactions and feelings surface; and by continuing to be a good listener, he allows the receiver the ownership of and the responsibility for her feelings.

Conversation

Families need to devote special time and attention to the revitalization of the art and pleasure of conversation. Since it provides an invaluable forum for affirming communication, time should be set aside for family activities that center around talking and listening: family nights for reading aloud and discussing books and current events; sharing time after school, work, or before bed to review individual reactions to the events of the day. These experiences provide opportunities, within the safety of the family, for everyone to increase his range of concepts and of vocabulary, particularly his knowledge of those words that can express feelings and emotions more accurately. In what specific way are we sad? lonely? hurt? How are we happy? ecstatic? pleased?

Families with young children can play games that involve the discussion of relationships and values. Social Security[5] is a cooperative board game that encourages sharing thoughts, experiences, and affirmation. As players travel around the board, they make stops at the Dynamite Solutions Juice Bar, the Feelings Fruitstand, the Values Market, the Parking Lot, and the Changing Stage, where cards pose thoughtful questions or invite affirmation or handshakes all around. *Helping Your Child Learn Right from Wrong*,[6] by Sidney B. Simon and Sally Wendkos Olds, is full of activities that stimulate fun and conversation, while exploring the process of clarifying a family's values. *Pass along Stories* is a game that teaches conversational skills, at the same time that it develops listening, imaginative, and descriptive abilities. It can be played with as few as two people and makes an enjoyable travel game. One person begins with a story, with a lead-in line or two, such as: "It was a cold and blustery fall night. I looked out my bedroom window and saw a dark cloud drift across the moon. Suddenly . . ." At this point the story is passed along, and each person adds something to it until time or the plot draws it to a close.

---

[5] Social Security, made by the Ungame Company, 1440 South State College Boulevard, Building No. 2D, Anaheim, Calif. 92806.
[6] See the Annotated Bibliography, pp. 176–77.

One major block to family conversation in our society is television. While vastly broadening the scope of our ability to exchange information, it can have a deadening effect on the development of our conversation and our proficiency to form relationships. Once it is in our home, the TV provides an ever-present temptation for companionship without hassle, effort, or back talk. For many people it has become a treasured companion that gives the illusion of communicating, while requiring nothing in return. It physically immobilizes, absorbs, and distracts us; some say it even addicts us. (Every parent who allows her child to watch TV should not only read but also discuss with her child Marie Winn's *The Plug-In Drug*.[7]) But TV is no worse in this sense than any other pastime that is used as a substitute for relating to or communicating with people. The fault does not lie in the lure of a good book, a tennis league, or a favorite TV show, but in our lack of commitment to trust in and share directly with people. It is not so much that we need to indulge in TV or other diversions less, but that we need to value our relationships with people more. We must take the time to listen, react, and express ourselves openly if we are to develop an affirmative sense of relating to others. If a family watches TV (sparingly we hope), it helps to do it together and then discuss what has been seen.

Through the experience of family conversation, each member can create a repertoire of blended styles of communication, which will expand his capability to relate flexibly and affirmingly both at home and in the broader community. Practicing the art of conversation can be both a means and an end to learning effective skills of communication. Through developing an aware and caring attitude, we can enhance our ability to send clear and positively stated messages, and to receive and accept information correctly in the same positive spirit. In doing so we affirm ourself and others and open new possibilities for understanding and personal growth.

---

[7] See the Annotated Bibliography, p. 177.

5

Emotions are a valuable human resource, a powerful storehouse of energy, which, when understood, accepted and clearly expressed, can fuel personal development and facilitate relationships. Since our feelings, as manifestations of our emotional energy, are part of what we are, they should be affirmed and welcomed as such, and put to constructive use in our lives.

All feelings are as natural and acceptable as breathing or blinking. Every healthy person is born with the potential to experience and express a vast array of emotion—joy, rage, anxiety, fear, hurt, anguish, and many others. Our feelings are shaped by the impact of physical and psychological stimuli. The individual (and largely subconscious) selection of an emotional response depends on our physical and psychological health,

Understanding and Accepting Our Feelings

the evaluative information that is available, and the extent to which we can confidently affirm ourselves and others. For instance, suppose you see a person walking toward you, swinging a blunt instrument. You are physically well and rational (not overwhelmed by feelings of persecution or anxiety). Because it is daylight and you are in familiar surroundings, you are able to discern that the person is a friendly, neighbor's child, carrying a baseball bat. Trusting yourself and the child, you might respond to the situation with a feeling of welcoming interest. The same incident experienced in the dark of night in unfamiliar surroundings, or by a person who is overwrought or physically defenseless, however, might trigger feelings of terror. We react because we experience; and our feelings, *all* of them, give a measure of the extent and quality of our perception of the environment and our relationship to it. Each of us has a responsibility to use our personal natural resources well. Feelings well expressed are indications of emotional energy well used. They help move us forward, give us information that we can use to help ourselves and others, and dissipate tension that is destructive to our physical and psychological stability.

Looking At Ourselves First

To understand and communicate our feelings in a clear and constructive way, we must become aware of and learn to identify the shadings of our vast emotional spectrum. We are inclined to describe our feelings nebulously as anger or joy, happiness or sorrow, hate or love; and to characterize them simplistically as either good or bad. In doing so we not only dilute the meanings of these descriptive words, but we paint a very limited and indistinct picture of our particular emotional tableau. In fact, most of our responses are a blend of a variety of feelings, and this meshing of many separate, yet sometimes not easily distinguishable, reactions is what makes it difficult for us to identify exactly what we are feeling and to know how to act on it. In the midst of an argument we might experience the mingled energy of indignation at being wronged, determination to get revenge, release at striking out, and guilt and remorse for getting even; rolling it all together, we might say that we are furious. Anger may include feelings of disappointment, anxiety, need, fear, rejection, and zeal, among others, and may assist or obstruct either personal growth or that of a relationship, according to the way it is communicated. Love may include feelings such as admiration, adoration, desire, need, protectiveness, and possessiveness; all of which also can either support or hinder a person or a relationship, depending on how they are expressed.

In the months following my father's death I found myself sorting through a jumbled heap of feelings that I had previously labeled only as grief. Emerging from my first reaction of shock and despair, I discovered within myself a kaleidoscope of feelings, which, unless I gave them appropriate attention, had the power to disorient and immobilize me. As the shifts in emotion became identifiable, I was able to befriend them and use them as guides to work through my sorrow. At times I felt agitated, anxious, confused. When these feelings took a firm grip, I found that plunging into some hard physical work, and letting my mind rhetorically echo the painful questions that plagued me, gave me release. When I felt nostalgic and yearning, it was comforting to look at old pictures and reminisce with my

UNDERSTANDING AND ACCEPTING OUR FEELINGS

mother. At still other times I felt an overwhelming loneliness that churned inside me until I sought out a quiet, safe place, where I could weep it away. There were feelings of frustration and annoyance when others did not share my mourning, and determination, commitment, and pride when grief might have stalled—but did not—the carrying out of most of my responsibilities; I also needed self-forgiveness and appreciation when I could not do more. Having made a conscious decision and effort to allow, accept, and attend to my responses, I was able to use them to benefit me and others. By being alert to the ranges of my emotions, by sorting out the ways in which I felt unhappy, sad, or upset, I could channel my emotional energy for constructive use—for healing and renewing.

People often characterize feelings like love to be good, and others like anger to be bad. In actuality all have the potential to initiate action that is either helpful or harmful. Feelings themselves are neither good nor bad; it is the way we use them that determines whether they will have a helping or harming effect. Certain feelings do convey either a negative or positive response to stimuli; that is, they are imbued with a sense of accepting (yes!) or rejecting (no!). Again, however, it is important to recognize that neither category has an inherently constructive or destructive intent or effect. An attitude of affirmation—the belief in innate goodness and the potential for unlimited growth—can shape the understanding and use of feelings so that they become catalysts for continued development. Broadening our ability to describe feelings more accurately encourages us to be more aware of the nuances of emotion; it enables us to communicate more accurately how we feel, and to identify what action we need to take. Refusing to label emotions as either good or bad allows us to use all feelings productively.

Without affirmation, the expression of feelings that are usually considered positive can be damaging. Love can be harmful if it stifles and inhibits personal growth; or limiting and smothering if it insists that a person remain too close and predictably unchanged, as when a mother would rather spoonfeed her three-year-old "baby," or a father arbitrarily refuses to allow his fourteen-year-old "little girl" to attend her school's Friday night teen dances. Even trust can have a damaging effect if parents give their children permission to engage in dangerous or excessive behavior, or when they are blind to a threatening reality. Some parents claim, "I don't have to put restrictions on my children. They are good kids, not the kind who get into trouble." Though in principle the affirmation is a sound one, it underestimates the desire of children to learn and explore; it overlooks the pressures and temptations of our complex environment; it side-steps the elements of concerned involvement, communication, and mutual education as necessary factors in supporting young people to make informed choices that will reflect their intelligence and goodness.

"Negative" feelings, if creatively channeled and well expressed, can have positive effects that encourage and assist personal growth. Anger can be useful if it makes us take action to counter injustice. Fear is helpful when it protects us from harm. Feeling and saying no can demonstrate concerned involvement and belief in human potential. A parent who feels upset about a young person's activities or values, and who can express his disapproval in a nonattacking way, affirms his child by indicating an openness to and respect for communication. A parent may tell her child, "I have noticed that your friend Bob has been acting strange lately; he seems distracted and withdrawn. I've heard rumors that he is using drugs. I feel nervous when you are with him, especially when you go out with him in his car." Stating this concern in a nonaccusing way encourages the teen-ager to respond to his parent's worry and fear, rather than defend himself or his friend.

Perhaps his answer will be, "I'm worried about Bob, too, but I don't want to stop being his friend. I agree that sometimes driving with him is dangerous. When I know he's high, I make excuses and don't go in the car with him. I really want to talk with him about it, but I've been afraid to. I don't want him to make fun of me, or to think I'm acting strange. I'm glad you told me how you feel. I guess we'll both feel better when I decide how to handle it."

Another teen-ager might down-play his parent's concern by saying, "Aw, Mom, you're exaggerating. You just don't know what you're talking about." The parent's anger at being cut off and discredited in this way would be a likely and understandable reaction. That anger appropriately expressed, however, might clarify for both parties the intensity of the parent's fear and the depth of her need to know what is happening. Nonattacking anger is an effective way of communicating frustration and of insisting on being heard and taken seriously.

In fairness to her viewpoint the parent might reply, "Hold on! I'm telling you that I feel afraid! Since that affects how we get along, you need to know it. I agree that I don't know what is going on with Bob, but I do know what I feel when you are with him, and I need to get that out in the open. I want to know what really is going on, and how you feel about it."

This sharing of concern might clear the air enough to provide an opening to discuss trust, peer pressure, addictions, or other issues; it might lead to some active problem solving; or it may identify a problem that will require additional, long-term work. The concept of affirmation includes the constructive communication of both positive and negative feelings as a necessary part of mutually nurturing relationships.

In our society there is a vicious cycle of fear and suspicion concerning feelings, which springs from a lack of knowledge about them. We often treat our emotions like alien qualities—unfamiliar and mysterious, even threatening. By avoiding them, blocking them out of our conscious existence, we hope to steer clear of any influence or inconvenience they might bring to bear on the order of our lives. When a child is cranky and whines, we act quickly to distract or soothe her, as if by eliminating the behavior we dissolve the emotion or the cause of it. This simplistic approach can actually complicate and compound the problem. If the child's crankiness is just a sign of boredom, redirecting her attention may alleviate it. If, however, the boredom has churned up feelings of frustration or rejection stemming from some deeper sense of insecurity, distracting the child may curb the whining, but it may also push to the background the deeper feelings that still need to be expressed and given full attention. To dispel the uncertainty and anxiety that feelings often produce, they must be confronted, accepted, scrutinized, and when possible befriended as contributors of information and new dimensions of awareness.

Emotions Need Outlets

Emotional energy is kinetic, in that it determinedly seeks a form of expression, if not in words or thoughts or overt physical action, then in an internalized physical response or an adjustment of mental attitude. It may actualize itself in a frame of mind, such as contentedness, agitation, or depression; the emotions that produce that mind set might be further expressed by tears, shaking, laughing, yawning, or by involuntary physical reactions, such as hives, stomach upset, or fainting. The feelings may sweep into a more deliberate, outward expression, such as a temper tantrum, a hug, or a punch in the nose. The expression of emotional energy either dissipates it or initiates further action. If destructively communicated, it damages things and often people; if repressed, it can accumulate, shift, distort, and create tumult like an overworked pressure cooker. Our emotions comprise a moving, often turbulent, force that needs to be constructively channeled.

When my youngest child was nine months old, he was hospitalized with influenzal meningitis. Unconscious and near death, his pain was so great that the slightest touch caused him agony. For days there was literally nothing I could do for him but sit by his crib and pray. Keeping my composure was the key to being allowed to remain by his side, but my feelings raged through my body just as the fever and pain raged through his. My feelings demanded that I *do* something. I assigned myself jobs, like timing the drip of the intravenous to be sure it was working properly, talking and singing to him in the hope that he could hear and understand how much I loved and needed him to live, and eventually directly confronting his pain by assuming the jobs of temperature taking and diapering. These tiny ventilators for my feelings seemed insignificant in the face of the enormous fear, grief, and guilt that churned inside me; but they kept me going and were encouraged by the wise doctors and nurses who were more aware than I of the dual healing that was occurring.

Whenever I was coaxed into nibbling a meal in the hospital cafeteria "to keep my strength up," I was instantly stricken with severe stomach pains. When, late at night, I was forced to go home to "get a few hours' sleep," I could only sit in the darkness and cry endless, silent tears. Holding on meant holding back, but the feelings had to go somewhere. Miraculously Gregg was completely healed. He got all the attention he needed at the very time he needed it. For me, however, the healing is still in process.

Even now, fourteen years later, when Gregg catches a cold a remnant of the old fear comes creeping back like a specter to haunt me. I want to put him to bed, lock the doors, and keep a silent, restless vigil until he is well. Again I feel caught between controlling my fear so that it doesn't afflict Gregg, and acknowledging and releasing it so that it does not harm me. At these times, in the reassuring presence of a support person, I can still cry to dispel the stored energy of those old feelings still deep inside me.

Feelings Initiate Change

Perhaps it is because we sense or know that emotions can initiate action that we feel so uncomfortable about their expression. When feelings surface, they carry with them the suggestion of unpredictability: The prospect that things are going to change is disquieting to us. If a person begins to shout or to cry, she or others around her who are depending on "solid, clear-minded behavior" may feel that their security (at least their *status quo*) is threatened. Sometimes, anticipating change, we try to prepare ourselves for it by predicting what the change will be. If a person has experienced anger that has resulted in destructive behavior or physical harm, for instance, he may subconsciously conclude that all anger means that danger is imminent. When he senses that anger is building and that the relative peace of the moment is about to be shattered, he prepares for (and acts as though he expects) the worst. This second-guessing may actually guarantee the anticipated results. When feelings like anger are accepted as normal, and when they are expressed confidently without menacing or attacking others, their energy can be channeled so as to produce clearer evaluation, the productive exchange of information, and positive action. Acknowledging and revealing feelings may jiggle us out of our complacency or comfort, often with rewarding results. If we are forced to re-evaluate issues and relationships, we may then keep them fresher and more nurturing.

Expressing Feelings Acceptably

Young children allow their feelings to operate as a natural function; they do not question their validity or appropriateness. They manifest both positive and negative ranges of emotion without compunction. In fact, they usually let out their feelings—joy, hurt, frustration, and all others—with zeal, enthusiasm, and ardor. They ooze satisfaction when they have accomplished something. When they are angry they wail and flail it out of their systems and then go on with their lives, feeling renewed. In doing so, they sometimes hit upon a means of expression that rather than constructively directing their emotional energy uses it to hurt or damage. When their method of communicating draws disapproval or retaliation, the initial feelings become entangled with others, such as failure, guilt, and rejection. A two-year-old struggling with sibling rivalry may vent his jealousy by biting. For a person who cannot yet reason extensively or who doesn't have an expansive vocabulary, biting literally makes the point: "I feel hurt because of you; now you feel hurt because of me." If the child is interrupted and told, "I know you are angry, but you must not bite. Biting hurts," the child might repeat the biting because it accomplishes his purpose: "Right, biting hurts. That's just what I was after." The child chooses a course of action that seems to get his needs met. If the attention that the child craves can be secured only by biting, or by the subsequent methods of punishment such as spanking or scolding, the method still works.

When the way we exhibit our feelings discourages positive attention or constructive problem solving, the behavior should be interrupted and a new one taught to allow disclosing feelings that will lead to a more positive result: "Carol, if you are so angry that you want to bite, bite your blanket or an apple, but don't bite people! If you are angry with me, tell me about it and I will listen [see Attentive Listening, pp. 63, 141]. If you are angry with Jason, I'll sit with you while you tell him about it [see Supportive Presence, pp. 128, 170], or I'll make believe I'm Jason and you can tell me off [role playing]; but you may not ever bite people."

Children need help in developing their emotional resources healthily and productively. They need to be taught that all their feelings are natural and acceptable, and encouraged to express themselves in ways that are not destructive. To do this, adults must themselves learn to express their own feelings confidently and openly in constructive ways. A child will experience confusion and guilt if his parent tells him that it's all right to cry, although the parent himself never does; or if a parent angrily spanks a child, while disregarding his own advice: "I told you no hitting! You'd better learn to control your temper!" Expressing feelings openly and ac-

ceptably is an important function for people of all ages. Truly accepting and valuing emotion as a human resource and acting consistently with that belief is an essential part of nurturing and being nurtured.

As we grow up we get ambiguous messages—directed by conflicting attitudes about age and sex roles—about what are appropriate outlets for feelings. These acceptable outlets become increasingly channeled by social pressure to adhere to stereotypical role models or popular psychologies, while our accumulated personal experience and understanding of our emotions becomes more complex and intense and may develop along another route. A grownup who displays his or her feelings freely in public is sometimes considered weak and vulnerable—an easy mark. A person who doesn't ever seem to show his feelings openly, however, may be considered hard or cold. For males, crying and hugging are eliminated at a very early age, while punching or tussling are considered normal almost indefinitely. Females are allowed tears throughout their lives, but as they grow older, must learn to cry discreetly if they wish to be considered "mature and well balanced." Anger is acceptable from adult females only if it is expressed in a way that stops short of physical aggression. Some adults, when forced to seek more sophisticated outlets for feelings, use sex as an emotional catchall.

When an adult outwardly displays emotion, it is often considered a sign of "falling apart," or losing control. Women, who have usually been given more social permission during their growing years to show their feelings, are frequently considered a weak link in the professional world, where self-control is a revered trait. The fear is that a woman might "cave in" (show emotion and ruin things) under pressure. This kind of faulty logic considers emotional reactions to be abnormal, assumes an extreme and irrational behavior without regard to the individual personality, and projects an unreasonable expectation of doom. It is true that extreme emotionalism—when a person is not rational or no longer feels that he has control over his feelings—may be a sign of a breakdown, just as the lack of emotionalism in extreme may be, too; but the balanced, constructive communication of emotions is a responsible use of information and energy, directed toward continuing development. Through the example set by adults who constructively make known and accept feelings, children can learn to use their own emotional energy for personal growth.

Expressing emotion is a natural process that must and will happen in our lives. Through the understanding and constructive communication of feelings, we convert emotional energy into positive action. Sharing feelings with others can bring insight about our own behavior and the dynamics of our relationships. The acceptance of emotion and the consideration of what it can tell us about our behavior and the needs of others can lead to re-evaluation and the resolution of conflict. Expressing feelings will then lead to growth.

Dealing with Feelings, Rather Than Demonstrating Them

When dealing with feelings, a fine line exists between developing emotional health and growth, and simply getting attention or action by displaying emotion. Like a flashy window treatment, feelings are sometimes arrayed to lure attention and extract a desired reaction. When there is no intention of, or commitment to, using emotional reactions as a basis for actual, honest work—as responses to be shared, understood, evaluated; that allow mutual insight or require work toward resolution—they then need to be identified and confronted as behavior that involves "acting out" or "demonstrating," and should be addressed as nonproductive, even damaging.

Demonstrating feelings inappropriately undermines trust and co-operation and evades the responsible acceptance of feelings. It sets up a barrier to understanding by drawing attention to the presentation of the feeling instead of to the emotional issues behind it; for example, a person who always whines or cries to get what he wants may eventually be ignored by people who resent and won't submit to emotional blackmail. Acting out feelings is often manipulative; it puts pressure on *others* to change: "Do what I want, now!" and is often manipulative, rather than positive, in that it fails to offer an opportunity for insight, dialogue, and the possibility of mutual change. When emotion is expressed in a way that is meant to pressure or inveigle, it should be interrupted, addressed, and redirected.

If six-year-old Mary whimpers whenever she wants something, her mother might interrupt this behavior and say, "Mary, if you need my attention while you cry, I will hold you, or if you need to talk to me about something, I am willing to listen. But I can't understand you when you whine. Which do you need to do?" It may take some repeated testing of this affirming but resolute stand before the demonstrator feels sure that she need not overdramatize or manipulate in order to be heard.

The demonstration of emotion should not be ignored, because the behavior may be an indicator of deeper feelings and needs that must be addressed, or simply a sign that the person has learned that emotional manipulation is an easy way to get what he wants. Either way, the behavior undermines healthy relationships and self-esteem. Demonstrating or acting out not only interferes with getting support, but also distracts the demonstrator from gaining insight and using it, and his emotional energy, to fuel responsible action. When feelings are acted out just to secure action, for example, using tears, anger, even playfulness or affection to get something; or attracting attention but refusing either to share feelings honestly or to make an attempt to solve the problem, the behavior should be gently but firmly interrupted, and an indication given that shows not only acceptance of the person and his feelings but also a willingness to work out a more positive means of communication together.

Expressing emotion involves the struggle of self-scrutiny and the risk of public vulnerability. When feelings are honestly, nondestructively, and nonmanipulatively aired out of a desire to seek clarity and release from emotional tension, it is courageous, hard work that affirms trust in oneself and in others. Awareness of feelings enables us to understand our own perceptions better, and to share them with others. We should choose modes of disclosure that serve these purposes well, that are adequate and appropriate—not merely polite or constrained, but truthful, illuminating, and nonattacking. And, as we learn to express ourselves more appropriately, we need and deserve affirmative support.

Accepting Other Peoples' Feelings

Accepting emotion entails affirmation. By welcoming the open, constructive sharing of feelings we convey an understanding of and appreciation for the natural process of putting emotional energy to work. By providing caring, nonjudgmental attention, we can help people and our relationships with them grow.

When we offer acceptance and affirmation of another's feelings, we need to remain aware that they belong to the person expressing them, that they are the reflection of his life experience and values. It is the owner, or sharer, of the feelings who has the responsibility of evaluating and acting on them. The supporter's responsibility, on the other hand, is to demonstrate his acceptance of the feelings—negative or positive—and to acknowledge their validity to the person who owns them.

Supporting and accepting negative feelings is a harder test of affirmation. The important work of releasing anger may be more easily accomplished if the supporter remains physically nearby, provides caring attention and an attentive ear, suggests an acceptable physical outlet for negative feelings, such as walking, running, or punching a pillow, or finds a setting where the person can scream or cry his feelings out without intimidating or being inhibited by others. Giving this kind of support consistently teaches that feelings are important and worthy of attention.

If the owner confronts us, as listeners, with negative feelings about ourselves, we must remember that these feelings do not necessarily represent us, but rather the owner's perception of or reaction to us: "This is how he sees me or feels about me, under certain circumstances, or when I behave in a certain way." Being told "I hate you!" does not necessarily mean that we are unlovable or unloved, but that love is not the person's response to us at this point. Even when feelings are destructively communicated or hurtfully suppressed, it is the harmful action of destruction or suppression, not the feelings themselves, that should be interrupted, disallowed, and when possible redirected into constructive expression. To face and make constructive use of negative reactions to us, we must accept those feelings as real to the other person, and, as much as we can manage, affirm that person for his courage and honesty in putting his feelings on the line. Then, with an attitude of self-affirmation, we may seek to discover what in our own behavior and in the needs of the other person contributes to his response. Only then can we evaluate and negotiate what changes need to be made.

Ironically, although we all deserve and seek affirmation, when people express positive feelings about us, we often feel uneasy. Sometimes we are embarrassed, unsure of what is the proper way to reply. Other times affirmation wakes feelings of denial within us: "I'm not that good. I don't deserve that." Occasionally we worry: "Uh oh, what's coming now? What's expected of me?" Again it is helpful to remember that the other person's feelings about us belong to that person. They indicate his or her perception of us. We have the opportunity to learn about ourselves by hearing how we make others feel, but only we can finally know whether the way others see us is the way we really are. Ideally, we will be able, if necessary, to make the two into one.

6

As we grow we need to be continually defining, appraising, and affirming our basic values as positive, guiding elements in our lives. Our values are the course determiners for our actions; they are the core beliefs about which we have deep feelings and out of which come guidance and direction for our behavior. Our values determine which friends, occupations, and possessions we seek and how we use our resources in pursuing and maintaining them. Strong, weak or ambivalent, they are communicated in all that we do and say.

Clear values give us a sense of positive direction. As we expand our personal skills and knowledge, we must also broaden our understanding of the values that direct their use. Affirmation of our strengths and successes depends

Values: Guideposts for Our Lives

upon identifying the value guidelines that we intuitively apply to decision making. We must also seek to determine how we limit our own growth and effectiveness, and that of others: sometimes we do it unknowingly, by clinging to values that do not truly belong to us, or by disregarding those that might challenge us to grow. Well defined and understood personal values provide a base for positive action. We can claim them with greater self-assurance, communicate them more effectively, and, sure of our own ground, become more aware and accepting of values that are different from our own.

Each person's system of core values is like a fingerprint, as unique as that individual's personality and life experience. The influences of family, religion, school, neighborhood, and working environment may strongly determine the range of values from which a person may choose his personal code, but in the final analysis each individual can truly own and assimilate only those beliefs that prove meaningful and worthwhile in that person's life experience. Tailored by and for the individual, these proven, core values ultimately guide that person's decisions and actions. For each of us, in the course of our life there evolves a code of shoulds and shouldn'ts, beliefs that we feel compelled to stand up for:

Cleanliness is next to Godliness; My country, right or wrong; or Children are people, too! and beliefs that declare our bottom line: I cannot go to war; or Never lie! These concepts are identifiable as basic values, not only because they are prized, proudly displayed, and have been chosen freely from a range of possible beliefs, but also because they are acted upon openly and with consistency by the person who chooses them. People are able to analyze and clarify their values through the step-by-step process of prizing, choosing, and acting on particular beliefs and behaviors.[1] Our shoulds and shouldn'ts define what each of us stands for and against, what we will pursue or avoid. Our values become part of us; they form another, unique dimension of our individual personality and history. They represent our perception of life truths: what is important or essential and what is superfluous or undesirable. Our code of values is a measure against which we judge how we will act, what stands in opposition, and what support we need to seek.

Learning Values

Families are the initial and probably the most influential sharing grounds for personal values. The family is the source of most of children's basic values, and it is also where the most painful struggles over choosing and rejecting values usually occur. Intentionally or inadvertently parents do teach their own values to their children. They convey them through their actions and emotional reactions, by the standards and rules they attempt to set, and by the customs and traditions they build into family life. Whether a child learns and chooses the values of his parents depends on the personality of the child, the open-endedness with which the value is presented, and the veracity of the value to the child after measuring it against other values.

---

[1] Simon, et al., *Values Clarification*, p. 19. See also p. 16 and the Annotated Bibliography, p. 176.

Many parental values are easily accepted by children, because they prove useful, comfortable, and appropriate. Others are assumed at least superficially, either because a child wants to emulate or please the parent, or because the child knows of no other alternative. Some parental values, though, are eventually rejected and cast aside, because either the value itself or the manner of its imposition cannot be brought into agreement with the child's view of the world or perception of himself.

The process of weighing, testing, and sorting values is a lifelong business. We are forever our parents' children, and it is our nature to be measuring continually where we are and where we are going, against where we have come from. As our changing environment fosters a constant reappraisal of values, each of us brings new ideas and beliefs "home" to see how they stand up under the scrutiny of our most demanding, intimate, and, it is hoped, affirming jury—the family.

Many personal values are learned so early in life that people often grow up under their influence without ever consciously defining or evaluating them. Children observe how others (especially their parents) view things like time, work, play, friendship, religion, and so on, and often incorporate others' interpretation of these values into their own codes of behavior. Each of us learns almost by osmosis to respect and revere certain things, and to challenge and oppose others, with what seems like instinctive direction. We have a sense within us that some things just are right or wrong.

Much of our instruction about, and interpretation of, values evolves from our daily routines. In every family there are procedures, rules, and customs that subtly but firmly suggest which things are considered of greater or lesser value. For example, in many families one's place at the dining table denotes a values message. During my childhood our family table was set with my father's place at the head. When I got married and had my own family table to set, I placed my husband and myself at facing heads of the table, with the children at the sides. One evening I realized that whenever my parents came to dinner I automatically seated my father in my own usual, cohead place. I suddenly recognized why, whenever my husband or I was not present at the dinner table, the boys battled over having our places at the heads of the table. To them these represented the seats of power and status. I recalled the concept of King Arthur's round table, at which no one was ever at the head and supposedly no one valued above any other. After examining our custom's motive and message more carefully, I decided that, for me, reserving a place of special honor for my father had a meaningful significance worth preserving; but it was equally important to me to find new ways to communicate to the children the spirit of honoring and respecting them also.

Each of us must learn the skills of identifying and communicating personal values. Since our individual beliefs so dramatically affect our feelings and our actions, they have great impact on our relationships, especially within the family. When parents know and share their opinions accurately, those values are less likely to be misconstrued; and their children learn, by example, methods of clarifying and communicating their own values.

Examining and identifying a personal code requires conscious attention, openness, flexibility, and an atmosphere of affirmation. The Life Goals Grid, drawn from materials developed by Drs. Nila and Ed Betof, can help determine by whom, how, and when some of your personal values were formed and either accepted or rejected:

LIFE GOALS GRID

Goal	Who	How: direct or indirect	Age at which accepted	Age at which rejected	Underlying value

Fill in the grid, listing in the first column the goals that were set for you as a child. In the second column indicate who transmitted each goal to you (mother, father, grandparent, teacher, self). In column three note whether the goal was directly articulated or made known to you through nonverbal approval or disapproval. In column four record the approximate age at which you accepted this goal. In column five, if you rejected this goal, note at what age you did so. In column six indicate what you perceive as the underlying value represented by the goal.

Choosing a goal that you first accepted and later rejected, write a letter to the person who offered this goal to you, describing the insight or occasion that caused you to discard or modify the goal. Include this letter and the grid in your journal. If you do this exercise as a family or support group activity, take three to five minutes for group members to fill in the grid; then in groups of two or three share "one thing that surprised you about the way you set goals." If young people are a part of the group, tell and discuss the story of King Midas, who was granted his wish that all he touched would turn to gold—the thing he thought he loved more than anything else. The king's idea of wealth changed after he accidentally turned his beloved daughter into a golden statue. Allow a few minutes for the group members to reflect on a time when they wanted to have, do, or be something, but later decided against it. Ask for some volunteers to share their stories and tell why they changed their minds. Ask everyone to imagine that he could become anything at all. Give each person an opportunity to tell his wish.

Constant but Flexible

Values are not scientifically proven facts that are undeniably consistent for all people, for all time; they are basic beliefs that ring true for individuals during particular periods (sometimes all) of their lives. Values are learned primarily through observation and experimentation, and they are changed by our own evolving perception and sense of self. Basic beliefs stand firm for the individual, even when they prove unwieldy or unachievable. They are linked with feelings that provide a thrust toward fulfillment. A person who deeply values a particular moral principle feels compelled to work toward it, and to witness and attempt to effect it in his broader community. A clearly defined, basic value acts as a guidepost for one's course of action.

Affirmed values, however, must not become static or unresponsive to the affinity of other viewpoints. They must be lived, with a sense of evolving awareness, and that requires flexibility. As people develop and are exposed to new ideas, their values must grow along with them. For instance, most young children love being noticed. They wish to be seen, heard, and paid attention to, and they are frequently willing to use any means available—they will scream, whine, clown, tease, or do whatever is necessary—to achieve that end. As a child grows up, if his need for attention is reasonably met, it is likely that he will become more relaxed and less concerned about getting it at any price. He will still value attention, but will feel more confident that it is available. In time, as a part of natural development, children become less egocentric in their needs; they begin to be more attuned to the needs of others. As this occurs a child who values attention may begin to appreciate, and be satisfied with receiving, more subtle expressions of it; he may then value giving attention as well as getting it. If a child's need for attention is not met, he may come to value it obsessively and to pursue it imperiously, finally getting it (probably in a negative way) only when his need collides with the needs of others.

As we mature, some of our values may change dramatically, even be subject to complete reversals, as when a person experiences a religious conversion, or an enlisted soldier decides he cannot kill any more. Sometimes values are just outgrown, like shedding dependence for independence. Affirmed values reflect our potential for growth. They must be concrete enough to be defined, significant enough to stir our commitment, yet adaptable enough to develop and change as we do.

Flexibility in valuing is often most important when our choices are not between good and bad, but between bad and worse. Frequently we must make value judgments or act when we have only unsatisfying options; for instance, deciding what to do with a litter of unwanted kittens, or choosing between telling a painful truth and lying. Realizing that our intrinsic worth as human beings is separate from our value judgments, and understanding that we have the unlimited ability to work continually toward expanding our range and quality of choices (in areas like civil rights and women's rights, for instance), we must proudly make even choices that are unsatisfying and appreciate our courage in doing so. This attitude exemplifies, of course, the essence of affirmation: It appreciates the best possible action in the given circumstances and believes in and expects continuing development.

Feeling Our Values

Our basic values are invested with a great deal of feeling and are a source of pride to us. We feel protective of them, and when they are challenged, it is not unusual to feel affronted or put down personally. Our values are at the center of what we are all about. If other people are "for" something we oppose or "against" something we prize, the energy of our feelings stirs in us. We react with fear, determination, frustration, amusement, according to the clarity and intensity of our stand. When we feel our values strongly, we may lose sight of the fact that while those values are an integral part of our thinking and acting, they remain separate from our (or others') worth and potential as people.

When personal beliefs are unclear or unstated, we are forced to work on gut feelings, and to communicate values defensively, perhaps arbitrarily: "I can't tell you why I'm for [or against] it, I just am!" or "I just *know* I'm right." Sometimes strong feelings that pop up from "nowhere" actually emanate from values that have not been clearly identified intellectually: for instance, feelings of embarrassment or shock when we hear ourselves make a prejudiced remark; or when teasing or horseplay go too far and suddenly, unexplainably, we feel offended or humiliated. The feelings alert us to values that need to be identified and either claimed or rejected.

When our values are clear, our feelings are also more understandable, and likely to be directed into positive action, working toward mutual understanding and continuing insight. By first acknowledging and dealing with our feelings, we unveil the issues they surround. Then, even if we cannot fully embrace the value, we can still affirm it as having a basis and a purpose for its owner, and recognize the potential of people and their values to grow together.

Clearly and rationally defined values are owned *by* people; they do not do the owning.

Hidden values are often a source of conflict in our lives. Unknowingly we can overstep another's values limits and find we have landed squarely on her feelings. When Beth went away for the summer, her mother decided "to clean out her closet for her." When Beth returned, she was furious to discover that all her craft and fashion magazines were gone.

"They were old and collecting dust, and they were cluttering up your room!" her mother retorted.

"But Mom, they were my personal property, in *my* room!"

Angry defenses were thrown back and forth. It became clear that the mess created by the magazines had been annoying Beth's mother for a long time, though she had kept it to herself. When Beth went away, there seemed to be no mitigating excuse for the clutter. Mother did not value the magazines, but she did value her self-image as a tidy housekeeper.

The clash that resulted from her actions was an upsetting one. Beth's first reaction was to feel that her mother didn't value *her*, did not respect her rights of ownership and privacy. She felt as dispensable as the magazines. Moreover, Beth was hurt that her mother did not understand how importantly she counted her craft and designing work as a special part of her identity; she felt that her uniqueness was not understood and appreciated. From yelling and crying to explaining and finally negotiating, Beth and her mother had to work their way back from angry, hurt feelings to a solution that defined and respected their individual values. In the process they reaffirmed their love for each other.

All too often, though, values that have not been clearly identified or articulated can lurk beneath the surface of a relationship, unheeded, until there is an unexpected collision, sometimes with disastrous hurt and confusion. Even when values conflict, if they are identified, assessed, and evaluated openly, there is still an opportunity for people to affirmingly, respectfully, and lovingly disagree, while celebrating the uniqueness of individuals and their codes.

Clarifying Values

The development of strategies for the clarification of values has brought us new tools to use in identifying values. They are structured so that they do not imply a bias or a judgment about particular values. They are devised to make the clarification of values an objective and stimulating activity. As illustrated in the Values Posters exercise below, the strategies encourage looking at options: They invite people to claim their values, and focus attention on the repetition of attitudes and actions, and the subsequent emergence of patterns, that might indicate when behavior is guided by basic (but perhaps unclaimed) value judgments.

VALUES POSTERS

What do you value strongly enough to engage in a struggle or campaign for? Free speech? Animal protection? A shorter work-week? Have each participant draw a poster for his personal cause. Give each person three to five minutes to speak out for his issue. Hang all the signed posters in a "values gallery" (the kitchen, classroom, or meeting room). Each person should consider himself a spokesperson for his issue. At meeting times he may request to give, or be available for, an update on his cause. This responsibility ne-

VALUES: GUIDEPOSTS FOR OUR LIVES

cessitates keeping current on the issue and one's feelings about it for as long as the person chooses to publicly campaign for it.

Our values are a personal matter, but they are hardly private. They are apparent in all we do, and affect and are influenced by all the central groupings in our lives. We test and form our values wherever we are; for this reason, schools, religious groups, clubs, teams, and peer relationships have a responsibility to recognize, and be sensitive in exercising, their powerful effect on developing values. The process and example of clarifying and communicating sound values effectively is most important as a part of family life.

Through identification and effective communication of values, we invite understanding of our own motives and rules system, and we gain insight into the behavior, expectations, and needs of others. Sharing our viewpoints gives valuable information about when there is safe or common ground—as a basis for co-operation and support —and when there is need for dialogue, negotiation, or respectful distance. When beliefs are clearly defined and communicated, we minimize the possibilities for misunderstanding and conflict. By communicating our values openly, setting them out where they can be addressed, challenged, rebutted, or embraced, we become aware of their implications to our choices; we also become more in tune with our own commitment and patterns of consistency in supporting those values. By claiming our beliefs, we discover fresh resources and avenues for acting on them. Clearly defined, effectively communicated values form a starting point for positive action.

7 Before we ever join a club or religious group or sign on for a new job, we check out what the rules are to be sure we know and can honor the limits. When children join families, they don't have that opportunity. Even though from the beginning there are rules in existence, as part of each parent's internalized code of right and wrong, they are rarely set out (even between the parents) at the outset. They are only gradually uncovered, mostly on an as-you-go basis, often established as rules only after a child has transgressed.

In the beginning, of course, it is only logical that parents must articulate behavioral limits. Babies and young children have a limited perception of what is harmful to themselves and others, and even as they learn, need much practice in

Setting Positive Limits

deductive reasoning before they are able to conclude accurately, "When I do this, this happens, so from now on. . . ." Though children do not have the benefit of their parents' accumulated knowledge and experience, even the youngest have an instinctive sense of what feels comfortable and fair. Newborn babies know when they want to sleep or eat, and when they don't want to be awakened, held, or ignored. By learning about and taking those feelings and needs into account when setting limits, parents show their respect for the rights and needs of others, and a desire to work together with children to establish mutually beneficial guidelines. Including children in the process of limit setting gives them a chance to develop their skills in reasoning, making choices, clarifying, communicating, and acting on their own values, while considering the needs and viewpoints of others. It enhances their self-esteem and encourages them to become independent and responsible people.

Having clearly articulated rules protects people from harm and lets them know what is expected of them as contributors to the group. Establishing limits in a way that takes into consideration the individual personalities, abilities, wants, and needs of all parties, regardless of age, is an indication of respect; it invites cooperation, it demonstrates affirmation.

Positive Expectation

Limits that are stated in a positive manner, indicating trust and confidence, encourage a cooperative response. Mary Ellen, a nursery school teacher, reviews the limits that she has chosen for the class in an affirming way when she asks the students to tell her what is permissible before they go on a class trip.

"Children are so used to hearing our warnings about misbehaving. They always come up with, 'Don't stand up on the bus,' 'Don't yell,' 'Don't. . . .' I have to be very careful to respond in a positive way: 'I see, we should sit in our seats,' or, 'You're suggesting that we talk quietly? Can you think of something else we could do? . . . Yes, we could tell stories or sing!' It is so easy to say and think no or don't. We all need to practice thinking and stating the positive alternatives."

In another example, a parent might set a curfew but still show his trust in the integrity of his son by choosing to say, "Bye, see you at nine o'clock," rather than, "Don't come home late!"

Many times rules are made in response to an incident that has focused attention on what went wrong or what could go wrong. Waiting until a problem arises before setting limits causes the rules to be cast in a negative, even punitive light: "If you can't get yourself out of bed on time in the morning, there will be no TV watching at night!" Limits set after a problem or conflict has already arisen are often flavored more with distress than reason. Rules that are based in frustration or anxiety are likely to be repressive and retaliatory, and imply that a person is considered uncooperative or that her opinions and perceptions are not valued. The message is, "You are unable to judge what is right, only I can do that!" This kind of interaction can lead to a pattern of negative expectations and results.

Successful limit setting is best done in a positive, seeking way, before problems and conflict arise. The invitation to discuss limits can come from whichever party recognizes a new or changing situation that could cause conflict: "Now that I [you] want to go out socially with friends in the evening, we should take some time to talk about what we each need to be comfortable with that." The physical and emotional needs of both parents and child need to be discussed, as well as the moral and social values involved in the issue. Each person's feelings, values, and information should be carefully listened to and respectfully examined. Both parties have an obligation to become well informed on the subject before decisions are made. When limits are discussed in an atmosphere of caring openness and respect, the relationship will be strengthened and the partners affirmed.

Jamila, a bright, assertive eight-year-old who lives in a midcity high rise, was longing for some new responsibility and freedom. She asked to be allowed to ride the elevator downstairs to shop in the lobby store. Her mother agreed that Jamila was trustworthy and capable, but knew that riding unescorted in the elevator of the huge building was not safe for a young child. While discussing the problem, both had an opportunity to voice needs and feelings, and to begin planning together how the inevitable "getting free" could be worked out. Answering Jamila's initial request with a flat "No!" might have caused a conflict by making Jamila feel pushed to prove her right to independence. Because Jamila's mother took her request seriously as an invitation to discuss new limits, the two were able to negotiate a plan respectfully that would help avoid a crisis. Although the limit set for solo excursions had to be a compromise at first—going alone to a friend's apartment several floors down, when someone could meet her at the elevator—being included in the process of determining the limit showed Jamila that her opinions and good judgment were respected. Though still somewhat impatient with her limits, Jamila nevertheless felt reassured that she could initiate action and work cooperatively with her mother on setting limits that would reflect her growing maturity.

Since mutual limit setting frequently means compromise, it does not always result in everyone's being delighted and perfectly satisfied. Many times one or both parties may feel that the solution is less than what they hoped for; but when the process of negotiating limits is carried out sensitively and consistently, and people feel that their needs and concerns are being adequately reflected in the guidelines that are established, they are encouraged to accept compromise as a promise: to continue working toward increasingly satisfying, mutually defined limits.

There are four criteria for setting affirming limits: They must be negotiated, free of attached penalties or rewards, clearly stated and mutually understood, and kept current and flexible.

Negotiating Limits

When establishing affirming limits, both the values and the physical and emotional needs of both parties must first be considered openly and then perceptibly incorporated into an agreement. Establishing acceptable guidelines requires a process of negotiation. Just as the word "rules" implies oppression to many people, to some the word "negotiation" implies verbal harassment. Negotiation should not entail endless discussion, haranguing, bribing, or coercing. Negotiating limits should be a structured, rational process of examining the pros and cons of various approaches to a particular situation, then defining a mutually acceptable plan for addressing it. Negotiation needs to be a brief but thorough exchange, not an endurance contest. Carried out willingly and democratically, negotiation demonstrates good faith, self-confidence, caring and respect for others; it affirms both the individuals and the relationship.

With very young children, the responsibility of seeking to understand, interpret, and incorporate their needs into a program that sets limits falls primarily on the parents, and requires a great deal of sensitivity and a certain amount of mind reading. This kind of empathy and sense of fair play is evident in the parent who coos at a fussy baby: "I know you hate being all bundled up like this, but it is cold and rainy, and if we don't dress you warmly you'll get sick."

Often when talking to young children we use the inclusive "we" to signal our wish to embrace the child's needs in our limit-setting process: "Shall we put your toys away before we go outside?" This is an excellent way to practice and encourage a positive attitude of negotiating affirming limits. It keeps us mindful of working cooperatively with children to establish workable guidelines.

We must be cautious, though, not to convince ourselves that we always know what a child wants or feels he needs. As children mature, they become more able to formulate and communicate their own perceptions, and if we have become too smug or comfortable about predicting a child's needs (perhaps deciding that his choices will be the same as ours), we may be brought up short the first time junior responds to our rhetorical inquiry with, "No, I want to go out now and clean later!" Encouraged to speak their mind, given careful attention, and taken seriously, children can, as Jamila did, work together with parents to decide on limits acceptable to both. Certainly a newborn baby cannot verbally negotiate his bedtime, but he

can clearly communicate his need to sleep, and have input into his parents' decisions on setting limits. A four-year-old has the right and the ability to express her feelings—and have them considered—about whether or for how long she needs a nap; and a twelve-year-old can certainly put together a well-thought-out case for setting her bedtime at a particular hour. In all these situations parents should use their own knowledge and experience to complement the information offered by the child, in order to negotiate a wise and equitable arrangement. Both parents and children should be encouraged to assert their views confidently when establishing limits, but parents have to be particularly careful not to allow their position and power as adults to undermine children's cooperation. Older and wiser (and the unstated but obvious Bigger and stronger) is not an adage to flaunt or abuse, but an asset to share. How productively information is communicated and used depends largely on the extent to which parents exemplify and encourage the spirit of open communication and negotiation.

To begin the process of negotiation, each partner takes one or two minutes to outline his or her view of the situation: the behavior, its tangible effect, and the feelings involved:

"Recently you're often away from the house in the afternoon. I don't know where you are or when you'll be home. [behavior] It's a problem, because it's hard for me to make plans. Sometimes I want to do something with you, but you're not available. [effect] When this happens I feel frustrated, and I think that you don't care about being with me. Sometimes I worry that something has happened to you. [feelings]"

This situation could arise for either a child or a parent; and although no two people ever experience a situation identically, because they are unique individuals, in most situations there is generally some tone or thought that can spark empathetic support. While the explanation is being given, the listening partner must pay careful attention, and take inventory of the needs and requests being expressed. The listener should not defend or deny his actions, or attempt to give sympathy to the speaker. Doing so would sidetrack the process. Countering with "You do the same thing" is nonproductive and beside the point. Even though another person's actions may influence our own behavior, it does not alleviate or excuse it: Two wrongs don't make a right, as the saying goes. Though it may be useful, later in the discussion, to state how another person's behavior may have served as a guide to one's own—"I hear you use those words when you are angry, so I thought it was okay for me to use them," or, "I saw you throw that paper on the ground, so I thought you didn't want it any more"—interrupting and correcting, or meeting criticism with defensive countercharges will escalate conflict rather than aid in negotiating workable guidelines.

After the first partner has had her opportunity to describe the situation, the other should briefly restate what is understood. If that understanding is not refuted, the second partner can then describe what is happening from his point of view:

"Lately I have more free time and opportunities to do things away from home. When something important or interesting comes up, if we haven't made previous plans, I feel free to go. [behavior] When I get home and you act annoyed or lose your temper with me, [effect] I feel that I'm being treated unfairly. [feelings] I hadn't realized that you might feel afraid for me. I can understand your frustration when you want to go out or do something and my absence keeps that from happening. You seem to be saying that time together is important, and I agree with that. How can we work this out?"

At this point the initiator, too, might want to check her understanding of what has been said or suggested: "When I haven't been clear about what I expect, you're hurt and confused by my anger. We both seem to want some time together, as well as the freedom to do things separately."

Next, each partner must state what consideration each feels he or she needs, in order to determine mutually agreeable limits: "I need time with you I can count on, and I need to know that you are safe."

"I need to have more freedom to pursue new interests without upsetting our relationship."

Each partner must then state what he or she can contribute to arrive at an acceptable solution; then guidelines can be set: "From now on, I won't make plans for us without checking with you first.

Let's try to plan ahead for afternoon outings, and check the dates on the kitchen calendar."

"If I'm not going to be home, I'll let you know where I expect to be in the afternoon, and I'll be sure to be home at five-thirty. If something unexpected comes up and I won't be home on time, I'll call you so that you won't worry."

If a suggestion is not acceptable to one party, it should be addressed simply: "I'm not comfortable with that. Can we talk more about it, or think of some other ways to do it?" If it is thoughtfully expressed, it should be seen not as a rejection but as an invitation to search for a more creative alternative. Ideally there should be a broad spectrum of ideas to choose from.

Finally the agreement should be briefly restated and a time determined to check back on the progress of the arrangement: "We are agreeing to plan ahead and let each other know our expectations. You'll be home at five-thirty or call to let me know if you'll be late."

"Yes, that sounds good. Let's try it for two weeks and then talk again about how it's working out."

A limit that is arbitrarily drawn or discarded, because the needs of either party cannot be rationally supported, may close down communication completely on the matter, which will only create more conflict. Additional continued dialogue and negotiation are then needed. When communication about an issue results in real understanding and agreement, however, there is often no need for rules.

Penalties and Rewards

The attachment of penalties and rewards discredits the negotiation of limits and hinders cooperative, nurturing relationships. When negotiations are conducted in a spirit of affirmation, limits are established in good faith. The partners of a negotiated limit affirm their arrangement by asserting, "We are committed to a mutually acceptable management of this issue through the use of this approach." Attaching a penalty or reward to an agreement indicates an assumption that the rule is likely to be broken. If either party suspects this possibility, it is a sign that the limit has not been thoroughly or fairly negotiated, or that there is a serious lack of trust between the individuals that cannot be resolved by rule making. Placing restrictions—such as: "If you get home on time for a week, I will treat you to a movie next weekend [bribery]"; or, "If you don't come in on time as we have agreed, you will be grounded this weekend [coercion]"—implies an expectation that a limit is not workable, or that the person for whom the limit has been set is not able or willing to honor it. The fault lies in either the limit itself or the base of trust; and penalizing (getting even) or rewarding (paying off) does not build trust or compensate for unrealistic limits.

The use of penalties and rewards attacks the integrity and the self-esteem of both parent and child. Rewards taint the deserved honor of successes by making them feel bought rather than self-determinedly pursued and achieved. Responding to mistakes or faulty judgments with punishment or penalties sets up power struggles by advocating the use of force or manipulation to maintain control. It invites testing rather than trusting. Everyone loses in a power struggle, as the ante is constantly raised until the struggle itself consumes all the creative energy. When penalties and rewards are automatically attached to limits, it cues children in to the concept that for a certain price they have the option of ignoring the limit: "Who cares about a movie? I'd rather be with my friends now," or, "There isn't anything happening this weekend, anyway; I'll stay out tonight, instead." This disregard of guidelines can become a vicious cycle, carrying with it feelings of guilt, failure, and spitefulness, for both parent and child. The use of penalties and rewards is a method of externally imposed discipline rather than inwardly motivated self-discipline. It necessitates the involvement of an overseer, and it short-circuits the learning process by returning the burden of appropriate behavior to the enforcer. An emotionally healthy and stable person should be expected to and *will* observe reasonable and rational limits readily when he is convinced that those limits are in the best interests of himself as well as others.

Setting limits through negotiation is a process intended to develop personal responsibility and to open channels of communication and learning. An important part of this process is allowing people the opportunity to perceive the results of their actions, and to gain insight into the effect of their behavior on others. Unlike punishments or rewards, which comprise penalties or privileges imposed by persons of ''higher authority,'' these effects are the direct result of a person's own actions, they are never contrived or rigged.

It has been clearly agreed, for instance, that a child will be responsible for getting dirty clothing into the laundry hamper. If the clothing is left on the floor it doesn't get washed. There will be no prodding or reminding. Should the child let the clothing accumulate she will soon be faced with a learning situation. If a parent intervenes—''Jane will need clean socks tomorrow. I'll have to gather this up myself and wash it!''—this lesson is learned: ''This rule wasn't

very important; my comfort still comes first. If I forget the laundry, someone will take care of it for me."

On the other hand if parents arrange consequences to teach the child a lesson, no matter how kindly intended, they introduce an "I'll show you!" tone into the relationship. If, annoyed by Jane's forgetfulness, Dad hides her remaining clean socks in order to force Jane to put her clothes in the hamper—"That will teach her that we all have to take care of our responsibilities!"—he has decided and is communicating that neither he nor Jane are able to resolve their differences through direct dialogue. If this approach is repeated, Jane will eventually realize that Dad has thrown in the towel on cooperative problem solving, leaving her with little incentive and no partner with whom to negotiate.

In many families there are certain privileges, such as allowance, use of the family car, or trips to the candy store, that are commonly withheld as punishment or doled out as a reward. These niceties called privileges are held in a sort of escrow account, and when something unexpected comes along, are either given or reserved, depending on the situation. If Mary gets a D in English or is elected class president, she may have her allowance either cut in half or doubled, though there is no identifiable connection between the event and the response. Often no clear limits have been set on the use or regulation of these privileges, and because they are frequently items that parents have mixed feelings about—"I love candy, too, but I hate paying dental bills," or, "You should learn to handle money, but you spend what I give you on all the wrong things"—there is some unwillingness to negotiate and establish clear limits. They become catchall punishment and reward mechanisms.

One of the best twentieth-century examples is the privilege of watching TV. Because the effects of TV has been the subject of much heated debate, many parents have conflicting feelings about how much TV their children should watch. One thing is sure: Good for them or not, children (and many parents) love watching TV, and it makes an effective bargaining tool: "If you do all your homework now, I'll let you watch Animal World tonight," or, "If you don't stop whining, you'll go to bed without seeing Super Heroes!" This arbitrary and illogical use of gratification to control behavior is insulting and infuriating to children. It is a commonly used power play that is very destructive to family harmony, and a complete contradiction to the concept of negotiating affirming limits.

Instead of hoarding privileges to use as behavior modifiers, parents might examine the issues behind the so-called privileges, assess their own values in relation to these issues, form opinions, and discover through practice, discussion, and negotiation how the privileges can be used to strengthen and enrich family life. If, after careful scrutiny, parents discover that they are using a double standard by which to judge these issues in relation to themselves and their children (as is often the case with the use of TV, cigarettes, alcohol, drugs, etc.), they will have to come to terms with their own attitudes and practices if they hope to negotiate credibly fair and honest limits with their children.

If the negotiations have been conducted with complete candor and honesty, the limits will be based on the best information available to the parties involved. If there is no coercion or hidden intentions, no planned lessons to be learned, if both parties genuinely expect the agreement to be a workable one, it is likely to succeed. If, under these conditions, the limit is not manageable, it is probably because some factor has not been considered, or the situation has somehow changed. Placing blame is useless and counterproductive. The fact that a negotiated limit cannot be maintained provides important information about the situation and indicates that renegotiation is needed to achieve a truer understanding. Still the process of setting limits has succeeded as a learning tool, communication has become clearer, and the new information can provide a fresh starting point for renegotiation.

Openly and Clearly Stating Limits

Limits should be clearly stated and defined, in simple language that leaves no doubt of the expectations or promises made. For instance, setting a curfew as "early" is an invitation for interpretation. Be specific; agree on an exact time. If the issue is how many friends may visit the house at one time, agree on a number. If the record player is too loud, decide where the volume control should be set so that it is mutually acceptable. A lot of arguments and their reruns, as well as the need or temptation to make arbitrary decisions, will be avoided by being specific before there is real conflict. When a limit has been agreed to, it should be briefly restated to be sure that both parties have the same understanding, and it may be helpful to write the agreement down.

Some family rules are not clearly articulated because they have not been deliberately evaluated or carefully chosen. They are the personal, inscrutable property of individual members, the shadowy reflections of accumulated life experiences and subconsciously acquired values. These unnamed "musts" and "must nots" sometimes stem from a kind of hidden emotional baggage—worries, fears or hurts, or ingrained traditions or customs. When each member brings a certain number of these mysterious encumbrances to the family, the cumulative effect can be overwhelming. If there is no process or means of getting these taboos out in the open, where they can be objectively examined, much energy will go into second-guessing, shadowboxing, and sometimes even exploiting these vague restrainers.

The Rules of the System Grid, developed by Drs. Nila and Ed Betof, is a tool for identifying both the articulated and the hidden rules within a family, class, or other group, as they are perceived by the individual members. It is also a useful self-help tool for illuminating the limit-setting style of an individual. Responses to the grid may shed new light on what group members would like the rules of the system to become, and what needs to happen to make that possible.

After filling out the grid, note any patterns; for instance, do most of the rules meet only your needs or only your child's needs? Are there frequently consequences or penalties attached? Are there rules that are regularly by-passed, or that there are exceptions to? Has anyone been "strongarmed" in the negotiating process? And

RULES OF THE SYSTEM GRID

	Rules of System	Meets Needs of Parent or Child (or both)	Negotiated	Has Clear Conse-quences; Natural or Arranged	Is Maintained Consistently (Manage-able)	Stated in Clear, Simple Language	Is Common Knowledge to All
1.							
2.							
3.							
4.							
5.							
6.							
7.							
8.							
9.							
10.							

are the end results absolutely clear to all? Write a letter (which you need never mail) to one of your parents about a rule you have brought from your childhood to your present life. Tell your parent about a new rule or limit that you have created and are proud of. Include it and the grid in your journal.

Keeping Limits Current and Flexible

Remembering that one attribute of affirmation is the expectation of people's continual growth and expanding capabilities, affirming limits must be established, with the understanding that they, too, will change with the people and circumstances that they were created to serve. Change is an essential part of growth. As people and relationships evolve, behavioral codes should be constantly re-evaluated to see that they keep pace. Changes in values, circum-stances, information, and abilities affect the validity of limits that have been set. Family rules should not be collected and preserved like heirlooms. As they are outgrown they should be improved or amended, making way for new contracts, or no contracts, that celebrate growth, trust, and greater autonomy.

When children are very young, there is a real need for limits and rules to protect and guide them, but as knowledge, experience, and self-assurance increase, children must gradually cast off parental guides and establish their own internalized authority. In a family in which there is trust and open communication, in which the expectation of amending and eventually discarding outwardly imposed limits is implicit in their creation, there is an awareness and welcoming attitude toward young people's innovations and requests for change.

The passage of time itself demands flexibility in determining guidelines. Social standards—rules influenced by currently popular values—kaleidoscope through time, from bathing dresses to bikinis, as quick as you can gasp. Some people hold onto standards, or codes, as if by doing so they could hold back time. Others cast them off without a backward glance, hoping to be swept along with the tide. This disregard of a value's intrinsic worth, aside from society's judgment, is a sad waste. Values should never be asserted only for tradition's sake or scrapped in the name of progress. Each person needs to continually re-evaluate her beliefs in the light of their present truth, discarding those that no longer ring true, while seeking the courage to take a stand on, and the clarity to decide on, which issues she really values. Sometimes, when partners clash while negotiating limits, because of the differences in their value systems, it is important to realize that standards do change, and that what is most useful is to treasure one's personal values proudly, while respecting the right of others to hold different ones.

We are separate and uniquely different from our children. We must encourage our young to know and understand our values, so that acceptance and communication are possible; but we must also give them the liberty to test our values in the light of their own personalities and environment, trusting them to arrive at limits that demonstrate respect for the needs and values of those directly involved. Learning to communicate and negotiate skillfully allows one to step back from the emotionalism of an issue, and to examine the validity of the values themselves rather than challenge the worth or integrity of the individuals who hold them.

Setting limits depersonalizes the issues, so that the criticism is not of a child being judged good or bad, but of a standard—rationally and mutually defined—being proved workable or not. If the limit is not mutually acceptable, there is no need for a degrading punishment, only a call for renewed communication and a search for a better resolution. Setting limits affirms the capability and cooperation of children, as well as of parents. Inviting a young person to share his ideas about personal responsibility and the kinds of relationships he needs demonstrates confidence in his ability to think clearly and sensitively and provides an opportunity for him to develop and practice those skills. Determining guidelines encourages a feeling of responsibility to a larger social unit, and is a constant reminder to both parents and children that their behavior directly affects others.

As each person experiences the process of negotiating limits, his goal should be to develop the skill to assess and make decisions fairly and objectively. The effect of the process is that the family members learn to examine their own values and motivations, and to respond thoughtfully to those of others. The ultimate outcome is self-regulated, responsible behavior and the confidence and self-esteem that accompany it.

8

If I turned to you now and said, "I have a problem," and proceeded to describe it, what would you do? Trying to be helpful, you might sympathize: "Oh, you poor thing"; or deny: "It's not as bad as all that"; reassure: "I'm sure it will blow over"; or reminisce: "Well, when that happened to me. . . ." You might relish the role of a confidant: "Oh, really? Tell me more!" or feel uncomfortable: "I don't think this is any of my business." Yet, whatever your response, you would probably wonder: "What's going on? She writes and gives workshops about solving problems, and here she tells me about hers. What is wrong with her? Is she a hypocrite?" All too often, problems are seen as signs of personal inadequacy or failure. We work to keep up the façade that life is perfection, all joy and laughter; because admitting that we have problems feels like public disclosure of inadequacy, a confession that we do not measure up and something must be wrong with us.

Problem Solving and Conflict Resolution

Problems are *not* an aberration in normal life. But the expectation of perfection that we impose upon ourselves and our children *is* abnormal and even destructive. After viewing a TV situation comedy in which siblings decided that becoming "perfect" children would achieve their goal, eight-year-old Will turned to his mother, Karen, and said, "Mom, you'd like Sarah and me to be perfect like that, wouldn't you?"

Karen thought for a moment: had she really given him the impression that she wanted perfect behavior? True, sometimes it felt as if she wanted that, but if perfect behavior became the goal, what boring, shallow people they would be! She hoped for independence, imagination, and yes, pluck, in her children. Karen replied, "Sometimes I want you to behave differently, but that's not the same as wanting you to act perfect all the time. You are much more interesting and fun to be with the way you are!"

This chapter was written by Penni Eldredge-Martin.

Conflicts and problems are the acid test of our belief in affirmation. For while we may comfortably accept the theory and have tried to integrate it into our family life and relationships, when conflicts erupt, our knee-jerk response is frequently to fight, fly, or freeze: "fight" the issue with verbal attacks or a rigid formula; "fly" from the problem by ignoring, denying, removing ourselves, or walking away; "freeze" by becoming psychologically immobile, unable to act on or confront an issue in any conscious way. Coupled with anxiety, guilt, and ineptness, these reactions create barriers to solving problems effectively; but given affirmation, appropriate support, and adequate information and skills, people can learn to face problems confidently and to surmount them.

If we recognize that each person—ourselves and others—is his own best problem solver, dilemmas become occasions of opportunity, in which the individual's right to pursue his own unique solution can lead to personal growth. With affirmation firmly at the center of the resolution process, confrontation of issues, not people, takes place. The dynamics of a "me versus you" approach shifts instead to an attitude of "we versus the problem." People working together, valuing individual skills and abilities while seeking a mutual plan of action, can achieve restoration and insight, along with resolution. As concepts of right and wrong, antagonist and protagonist, disappear, the defused power struggle frees vital energy and imagination.

If we can approach dilemmas confidently, at the same time valuing the problem or conflict itself as an opportunity for personal growth and insight, we will experience arriving at resolutions as a process of affirmative, imaginative adaptation to the complexities of changing situations. Understood in this way, the process becomes as valuable as the solution. Rather than struggling over hard-and-fast rules or assumptions determined by age, tradition, or the most *au courant* formula, we must focus on personal strengths, characteristics, needs, and abilities as integral components of a process that will lead to eventual resolution. By working out the variables cooperatively, we can begin to form unique, customized solutions. Basic to this process is an attitude of good faith, the setting up of a model, and an acceptance of equality of viewpoint, which is recognition of the fact that there is seldom one *right* answer.

Jean, eleven, had been in three different foster homes for a total of nine years. When she arrived at the Parkers', it was not long before a serious problem became evident—Jean wet the bed every night. The caseworker had never mentioned it. Each morning Jean appeared in the kitchen, sullen, damp, and angry. Nan and Pete Parker decided that her incontinence and the resulting feelings and extra laundry were a shared problem. They discussed the problem with Jean and together generated a list of possible solutions. Finally a mutually agreeable plan emerged. First, Jean would not drink any liquids after 8 P.M. For two weeks an alarm was set to ring at 2:30 A.M. Pete agreed to make sure that Jean got up and went to the bathroom. The following two weeks Jean set the alarm and was on her own. She agreed to be responsible for any extra laundry resulting from an accident; as long as it was washed, dried, and put away, no one in the family would mention it. Within a month, by the family's affirming and supporting one another, the incontinence, angry feelings, and extra laundry were overcome. This process allowed Jean to experience herself as responsible and capable of dealing with problems.

Positive expectations, or faith in oneself and others, is central to the process of solving problems affirmatively. It entails merely acting in concert with the belief in each person's capability and innate goodness, and depends upon the assumption that each person will be responsible to and respectful of the process and its outcome. Attaching punitive or disciplinary consequences as a solution to curbing unacceptable behavior calls into question a person's integrity and suggests: "If you fail to live up to our agreement, I still hold ultimate power to judge what's right or wrong and dole out results accordingly." Such actions or intimidations negate affirmation; they imply, in effect, "You must measure up to my standards," or, "There is a right answer—mine!" It is dishonest and manipulative to invite someone to enter into a process that promises shared responsibility, power, and support, if the bottom line is inequality of opinion and subsequent irresponsibility. Tangible, firsthand experiences in the process of resolution are essential to developing our abilities and sharpening our perceptions. Any suggestion that one party knows the right answer and will convince or finagle another into agreement will quickly short-circuit an affirmative approach. Often adults say to themselves, "But I don't want her to make the same mistake I did!" The urge to protect by seizing control of problems reinforces the stereotype that adults always know what is right, and leaves young people feeling inexperienced and afraid to attempt solving problems on their own.

Adults must exemplify their belief in the process of solving problems and resolving conflicts affirmatively by practicing it in their relationships with people of all ages. To do so we may have to "unlearn" some long-held assumptions about ourselves, children, problems and conflicts. If we are to experience and practice affirmation fully, we must begin to value all of ourselves, even those aspects of our lives that need improvement.

A Word about Process

Designing formulas for effective parenting has come into vogue recently. For the most part, these formulas are popular because they prepackage solutions. Having trouble toilet training your two-and-a-half-year-old? teaching your nine-year-old to clean up her room? or convincing your fifteen-year-old to be in by midnight? You can find a solution for each problem at your local bookstore. . . . As mentioned at the start of this book, the fault of these systems is that if they fail, the assumption is that *you* did something wrong. Little room is provided for personal quirks, abilities, curiosities, or foibles; past history, future goals, and family relationships are seldom considered. In other words, they are rigid, caught in the present, with no allowance for the wide variations of human experience, needs, or changing expertise. There is also the danger that these problem-solving methods may be seen as products of an exact, technical science to be learned by adults and "done to" children. Exclusive knowledge and use of such skills maintains the source of power with the adult. Power hierarchies and the manipulation that accompanies them are antithetical to a belief in affirmation. Teaching and learning methods and skills becomes much simpler if they are put into systematic, diagrammable formats; but when we practice these beliefs and concepts in our own lives, we must learn to improvise, expand, and extrapolate. Rigid methodologies are incongruous with the theory of affirmation, which emphasizes the appreciation of individual and situational uniqueness, and the innate potential for continuing insight and understanding.

The process of affirmative problem solving and conflict resolution is not so easy to package, for, like each of us, it changes to reflect individual growth, needs, and situations. The touchstones—equality, good faith, good example, and no "right" answers—all flow from the central concept of affirmation, of the belief in each person as his own best problem solver. This process asks more of us than simply following formulas, for as we enter into dialogue and accept shared responsibility for working toward resolution, we do not have the comfort of a preplanned result ahead of us. We are asked instead to trust, to value ourselves and others equally; the risks and rewards are greater.

Understanding Our Needs

Problems and conflicts, although they are similar, are not synonymous. Both share the characteristics of interrupting routine and jarring our expectations by introducing new, alternative, or contradictory information into a situation. The difference lies in the degree of this interruption. Problems are less severe and might be referred to as enigmas, puzzles or mysteries, questions raised for consideration or inquiring and possibly, a source of vexation.[1] Conflicts though, have a higher degree of tension caused by the collision of incompatible needs or drives.[2] Problems and conflicts can occur

---

[1] *Webster's Seventh New Collegiate Dictionary* (Springfield, Mass.: G. C. Merriam Co., Publishers, 1967), p. 678.
[2] *Ibid.*, p. 175.

within a single individual or between people. Problems arise when needs are unmet, conflicts when needs collide.

Basic needs, like sleep, food, clothing, money, and maybe exercise or entertainment, are easily recognizable. Needs for intimacy, support, solitude, commitment, or security are less tangible and are sometimes overlooked, misunderstood, or ignored. Each of us has a complex, ever-changing arrangement of needs that vary, sometimes drastically, within the span of a day, a week, or a lifetime; but whatever those needs are, they belong to us. We are responsible, therefore, *to* them as well as *for* them.

Unfortunately, needs suffer from the same bad press that problems do; somehow needs, particularly emotional ones, suggest personal inadequacy, and so we avoid announcing or asserting them directly. We expect those who care for us to intuit our needs correctly: "If he loved me, he'd know what I want for my birthday. . . ."; we take pride subjugating our needs, from a sense of obligation or duty: "I have a migraine headache, but I promised my sister. . . ." Though we generally guard our emotional needs like deep, mysterious secrets, we feel frustrated and angry when they are not understood and met.

Identifying and clarifying needs is complicated but integral to the process of affirmative resolution. Some needs are obvious, easy to recognize and understand: a parent needs to be able to walk into a child's darkened room at night without tripping on toys, or a child needs to sit near the window of the car because when he cannot see out, he gets car sick. These concrete, readily defined needs are the easiest to respond to.

Emotional and value-related needs are more subjective and may be harder to identify or to relate to: after school a young child may want a family member to greet him at the door because he is afraid of entering an empty house; or parents need children to knock before entering any closed door in the house, because they value privacy. In cases like these, it becomes very important to articulate fully what your need is, where it originates, and, if necessary, how others may specifically assist you in meeting it or lending support. If they are unable or unwilling to help you, your straightforwardness encourages a reciprocal honesty that sets the stage for negotiation.

Stating, sharing, or making requests based upon our needs does not mean that they will automatically be met. Expressing our expectations, values, and limits can lead to growth and confidence in ourselves and others; but we must recognize that when our needs differ or are in conflict with the needs of others, they may present a difficult test of affirmation.

Sixteen-year-old Josh came home from a shopping trip with a "punk" style of jacket. Teased by his friends because he generally chose to dress very conservatively, he had decided that wearing something trendy would take some pressure off him. He wanted to feel more a part of the group; and besides, he thought the jacket was neat. When Josh's parents saw the jacket, they exploded. Alarmed by stories they had heard about the punk movement, the thought that Josh could be swept up in something they feared caused them to panic. Fortunately Josh and his parents communicate well with each other, and after the initial venting of alarm and frustration, they were able to clarify their individual needs: Josh's for peer acceptance and self-expression, his parents' for information and reassurance.

When problems arise between people over unmet needs, they may point to a difference in values. Recognition and careful articulation of disparate values can be a step toward if not resolution, at least better understanding and, hopefully, affirmation of the individuals involved. In the case of Josh's parents, they acknowledged that his record of good judgment and sensitivity to their feelings warranted their trust. Affirmed in this way by his parents, Josh could accept their open but respectful concern.

Naming Our Needs and Claiming Our Problems

When conflict or problems result from unmet or clashing needs, identifying whose needs are at stake defines where responsibility for resolution lies. Drawing on the concept of problem ownership, as developed by Dr. Thomas Gordon in his theory on Parent Effectiveness Training,[3] and emphasizing the affirmation of each person as his or her own best problem solver, we can clarify whose needs are unmet and assign, in a positive and supportive way, the responsibility for the initiation of conflict resolution. Gordon discusses ownership in terms of parent/child relationships almost exclusively, but the concept can easily be broadened to apply to any situation involving adults and children, or adults alone. As Gordon sees it, there are three possibilities for ownership: the problem is yours, it is another's, or it belongs to the two of you together (to your relationship).

When the problem is yours, the behavior or action of another person leaves your needs unanswered, creates a conflict with those needs, or infringes on your rights in some way. For example, your four-year-old daughter is spread out in the living room, playing with

---

[3] *P.E.T. in Action*, pp. 22–27. See also the Annotated Bibliography, p. 174.

her cars and blocks. Suddenly, unexpected guests arrive. You would like to entertain in the living room but feel uncomfortable about the clutter and noise. Your daughter is quite happy playing; her needs are met. It's *your* problem in that your wish to sit and converse in a neat, quiet living room is interrupted by your daughter's playing and the clutter of her toys.

When you are an observer or confidant in a situation, with no direct needs involved, the conflict belongs to someone else. Circumstances are such that this other person's needs are being thwarted or interfered with by a third party. For example, your spouse feels let down and angry when the boss denies a request for a private office. In this case, it's your spouse's (another's) problem, since his or her needs for recognition and appreciation are unmet. You are not directly involved in the employer-employee relationship; your needs are not affected.

A third category emerges when your needs and the needs of others collide; you are in conflict. One or both of you have the strong urge to continue what you are doing despite the knowledge that this behavior or action prevents the other from meeting his needs. The needs of both individuals are endangered, and the problem belongs to you both, jointly—to your relationship. A case in point: your family has agreed to share responsibility equally for raising and putting up food. When the green beans are ready for harvest, you have a free morning to do the freezing and ask your ten-year-old son to pick the beans. He refuses, saying that he wants to finish the book that he is reading. Each of you is aware that your requests are troublesome for the other.

Identifying needs in a conflict can be complex. If unmet needs cause changes in behavior or the misplaced venting of feelings, chain reactions can occur that can compound, confuse, and even extend the problem. If, for instance, a person who is in conflict with another acts out his frustrations by blaming his family and friends ("It's all your fault," or "You don't understand!"), new problems may arise within those relationships. When we view problems as opportunities to confront needs and grow, when we learn either to accept or to surrender responsibility for them, the problems then become assets, in that they provide information and generate motivation. Obviously each one of us brings a differing set of expectations, history, interpretations, needs, and skills to any situation. In our diversity, whether from age or experience, lies a wealth of imaginative approaches and solutions to problems and conflicts; but we all must begin problem solving at the same point. By first identifying unmet or conflicting needs and establishing who should have the responsibility and opportunity to initiate the problem solving process, we can then gather relevant information and seek the skills and support necessary to put our problems to work for us. In this way, we set in motion the process of acting upon them rather than reacting to them. We affirm both problems and problem solvers as valuable resources.

As a volunteer on a hot line for battered women, I understood and agreed with the ground rule that we must not make decisions *for* the abused woman availing herself of our services; but the words sounded hollow at 6:30 A.M., the morning I met shaken, tearful, bruised nineteen-year-old Ellen (not her real name) and her two glassy-eyed preschoolers. Her husband had abused her for many months, but the previous night he had also threatened her and the children with a gun. My inclination was to gather them into my arms, take them to my home, tuck them in bed, and send the police after her husband. My agreement with Ellen, however, was that I would drive them to a safe home where they could rest, and Ellen could decide what steps to take next.

Two hours after leaving Ellen, I received word that she wanted to talk with me. She had called her husband, who was remorseful, especially after awakening to find her gone; and he had pleaded with her to come home, promising never to hurt her again.

"I think I want to go home, but . . ." She must have said it ten times, waiting for me to finish the sentence. Statistics, case histories, and horror stories whirled about me as I tried to accept the fact that the problem, the needs and values, were hers and not mine. I asked what she wanted, why she hesitated.

"Ellen, I can't tell you what to do. I'm not you. I can listen while you talk it through, but you must decide, because it's your life. You have to make the decision."

When I arrived to pick her up an hour later, I had to repress the urge to shake her. Instead, I shook myself. In her way, Ellen had done something drastic. She had left her husband, her home, her relatives. Maybe for the first time in her life she had made an independent decision. That had to be frightening, and for now, Ellen felt, enough.

Psychological profiles of abuse victims describe them as compliant and passive, internalizing the blame for problems and conflicts. They accept responsibility for any and all dilemmas but wait for others to resolve them. This description fits many of us, not just victims of abuse! The principles of problem ownership can help us distinguish whose needs must be considered and how we can appropriately satisfy them. By offering information and support while responding to Ellen's decisions, I affirmed her ability to make choices. While her choice differed from what I would have hoped, and raised questions and fears in my own mind, the central problem was hers.

Understanding, clarifying, and stating needs requires careful attention and shows our concern for others; it implies, "This is a relationship in which it is acceptable to think about and express what you need, even if it varies or conflicts with my needs." Misinterpretation, frustration, and guilt are less apt to occur in such an atmosphere. Accepting responsibility only for our own personal needs and problems, and sensitively designating the needs and problems of others to their rightful owners, can prevent new, related conflicts from developing.

Tools for Problem Solving and Conflict Resolution

As stated previously, problems and conflicts are not aberrations. Close attention to them can enlighten and enliven our interpersonal relationships by nurturing and affirming evolving abilities. Specific techniques, used to solve problems and resolve conflicts, are available that emphasize this possibility by incorporating good faith and equality into negotiation, and by eliminating expectations of one "right" answer.

Goal-Wish Problem Solving[4] is a useful technique for generating and exploring ideas from many sources when we must work on a problem that involves our own needs. When conflicts arise, family, friends, and coworkers show concern; they want to help, but too often this assistance comes in the form of unsolicited advice, reminiscing, judgments, and opinions. Goal Wish, a highly structured process, allows those concerned to act as a think tank by giving single-sentence responses to the dilemma. Acknowledged as the person best suited to resolve the problem, the owner is given the supportive attention and energy of those gathered, as well as the accumulated lists of ideas they generate.

When Edward wanted to go back to school but felt stymied by his work and family obligations, he gathered a group of friends together, stated his problem, then let the group brainstorm unlimited options for him. Selecting those ideas that seemed promising, Edward then named the weak point in his favorite idea, and the group set about brainstorming ways around that flaw. This Goal Wish process broadened Edward's thinking about his problem and allowed him to consider, without obligation, new possibilities for reaching his goal.

Conflicts within a relationship can be the most challenging, for they give rise to feelings of vulnerability and defensiveness. This type of collision of unmet needs traditionally becomes a test of wills, one person's sense of right versus another's. The power struggle that ensues can block any possibility for growth or learning. An affirmative approach, on the other hand, stresses an equal, mutual responsibility for the conflict, willingness and good faith in working toward a cooperative, satisfactory resolution, and a shared accountability for the results. The goal is to overcome or compromise on the unmet needs, not to overcome or compromise one another.

---

[4] For specific exercises illustrating this process, see p. 169.

Relationship problems often arise from faulty communications, expectations of intuitiveness, or the inability to identify and state our needs clearly. The *Virginia Reel*[5] is a structured, conversational technique, of unknown origin, which has evolved in Friends Marriage Enrichment[6] circles. A Reel allows owners of a conflict or dilemma to discuss the issue, with the support and objectivity of two other people. Their presence often defuses a tense interaction by interrupting the pattern of talking *at* and not *with* one another.

Wendy and Gary were workshop participants who expressed the feeling that something unsettling was afoot in their relationship. In a Virginia Reel they each had a chance to state the problem as it appeared to them and have it restated by an echo. During the first five years of their marriage Gary had worked part time and had taken charge of the housework and cooking, while Wendy had worked full time. With the arrival of their first child, the roles were reversed; but often, after dinner Gary had repeated Wendy's chores to meet his standards. Both had been quiet and tense when at home together. With the support of their Virginia Reel partners, Gary and Wendy were able to reveal their feelings of frustration, resentment, and guilt without assailing each other. Feeling safe in the presence of their unbiased restaters, they were encouraged to continue the process until their conflicting needs were clear. They gained valuable and needed experience in learning to express values and feelings, and to state needs in a straightforward manner.

In some conflicts the other party cannot be counted on as an active participant in problem solving. That person may not recognize that a problem exists—she may be unwilling or unable to acknowledge the conflicting needs—or she may feel unfairly challenged. While another's inability or unwillingness to respond may seem like a barrier to resolution, it need not be. By evaluating and changing our own behavior, thus taking responsibility for our share of the problem, we change the dynamics of the situation. By identifying our own

---

[5] See p. 172.
[6] For more information on Marriage Enrichment programs, write: Friends General Conference, 1501 Cherry Street, Philadelphia, Pa. 19102.

part of a problem and taking action on it, we overcome feelings of frustration, powerlessness, and hopelessness. Most positive feelings about ourselves, evidenced in visible changes in attitude or approach to a situation, can then encourage a cooperative resolution. Even if progress is slow or cooperation nonexistent, viewing the problem with greater clarity and objectivity will deepen our sense of self-esteem. Just knowing that we are *doing something* makes us feel better.

The *Turn-Around Problem-Solving*[7] method makes us feel more in charge of the situation and helps us cast off our personal image as victim. Initially the problem solver may choose to work through Turn-Around Problem Solving in the presence of an Attentive Listener.[8] Alerted to the steps of the process, this confidant can help the problem solver keep the process on track, by gently reminding him which step must be considered next: defining the problem solver's role in the problem; identifying the feelings involved; noting how the problem solver is invalidating or negating himself; and finally deciding how that invalidation can be turned around to self-affirmation and positive action. Once learned, this process offers an independent, step-by-step approach to problems that we might otherwise feel are impossible to tackle by ourselves.

Laurie, a high-school student participating in a teen workshop, told of feeling frustrated because her mother frequently arrived late to pick her up after school: "I need to get home. I have things to do!" Laurie felt the victim of a double standard, since her Mother certainly expected not to be kept waiting in the same way. When Laurie complained, her mother bristled.

"You don't seem to value your time that much when you talk on the phone and watch TV, leaving your homework until the last minute!"

After defining her problem in a Turn-Around Problem-Solving session with another workshop participant, Laurie recognized how her own double standard contributed to her problem with her mother. She often behaved as if her time weren't important, and now she

---

[7] See pp. 168–69 for additional information about this method.
[8] See pp. 33–35 and 141 for information about Attentive Listening.

was feeling that *she* was unimportant to her mother. She decided to turn her thinking around: "I am important! My time is important!" As a first step she planned to begin scheduling her time at home more conscientiously. She felt confident that this would help her mother see and respond to her in a different light.

As a caring observer to another's problem, we can demonstrate affirmation by giving appropriate support and encouragement to that individual, so that she can find her own (not *our*) best answer. When frustration, insecurity, and tempers flare, people often fall back on inappropriate responses. Many times young children, inexperienced in problem solving and unsure of their own intellectual resources, are tempted to slug it out for a fast and easy solution. Even adults, when emotions run high, will resort to snubbing, sniping, or suppressing, rather than confront a co-owner of a problem face to face. In situations such as these, a third party can be most helpful as a *Supportive Presence*.[9]

Chris and Lisa were having a heated tug of war over an unoccupied swing, when Jeff found them and gently but firmly separated them. Lisa, the larger and more assertive of the two, was shouting and threatening. "You can't have that swing—it's my turn!" Chris was tearful, and though obviously afraid of Lisa, looked determined not to give in. Jeff took the two girls by their hands and led them to a bench in a remote part of the playground. He told them, "I'm going to sit here with you and be sure that no one hurts the other. No hurtful words or actions! But you two must come up with a solution." He resisted Chris's pleading looks for intercession, and ignored Lisa's stubborn insistence that she or *nobody* was going to be next on that swing! Wanting to get back to playing and finally realizing that Jeff was not going to solve the problem, the two girls eventually negotiated a mutually acceptable plan for sharing the swing.

In a somewhat similar situation, between two adults, Gretchen and Tom found that friction because of conflicting views of their job responsibilities was making it uncomfortable for them to work to-

---

[9] See p. 170 for an explanation of this technique.

gether in the same office. Both really wanted to get things out in the open, but because of the backlog of hostility and misunderstanding, were fearful of a one-on-one confrontation. Harold, an aware and respected coworker, offered to sit in as an observer (a Supportive Presence) while the two laid their cards on the table. His presence created a feeling of safety that allowed them to share openly.

Conflicts and problems will remain with us throughout our lives; they cannot be eliminated and will seldom be easy to deal with. As milestones of transitions, calling for change and compromise, problems will ever be accompanied by a wide range of feelings and needs, testing repeatedly our ability to accept and act upon the concept of affirmation and the belief in each person as his own best problem solver. But if we can look on, even come to welcome, such dilemmas as opportunities for growth and the development of skills and resources, we will begin to form constructive attitudes and will share tangible experiences in responsibility, perception, and support. The present and future lives of our children, as well as of ourselves, will be enriched and affirmed.

Part Two
From Ideas to Action:
A Workbook of Projects
and Possibilities

A journal is an excellent tool for learning more about the people in your life, particularly the main character, you. A journal provides a means of "discussing" a concept without the actual presence of listeners. It is a tool for *intra*personal evaluation and problem solving.

The process of journaling, as it is suggested in this book, is a rather informal one—it involves keeping a free-flowing record of feelings, reactions, observations, and ideas, to give them growing room outside one's head: "I wonder if . . . I notice that . . . I feel . . . I suddenly realized. . . ." These stirrings of seeking and understanding should be recorded without analysis or censorship. There should be no "push" for resolution or interpretation; rather they should

Keeping a Journal

be kept as an unjudged stream of consciousness. Since truth is not static, new meanings and cues continually emerge as we review these notations of the inner dialogue always in process between our conscious and subconscious self.

Though it is a good discipline to try to achieve some regularity in using the journal, it should not become a mechanical process. Entries should be made "as the spirit moves us"—whenever we feel stirrings of concern or frustration or curiosity, when we have a moment of insight or of complete confusion, whenever an event or interaction seems for some special reason, or for no apparent reason, to be worth remembering. The journal should be used for capturing and chronicling events, feelings, and perceptions, in order to better understand our lives' progression. The purpose is more to evaluate than to analyze, and never to judge, since all that we think and feel is valid, useful, and important in the process of getting to know ourselves and our environment. Keeping a journal affirms the value of our thoughts by making them specific and by preserving them. It can be used to maintain a dialogue with one's inner self, tracking patterns and progress, and clarifying needs and goals, through the definitive process of recording them on paper.

Journal keeping also eases spoken communication. It can be a practice area for conversation with people we cannot, because of anxiety, hurt, separation, or for other reasons, presently address in person. By furnishing, in dialogue form, the responses of the other person (as we perceive they might be), we set down information about the roles we cast that person and ourselves in as we interact. Possibly the dialogue may also clarify how we would ultimately like the relationship to function, by giving clues to the action needed to be taken.

As a group tool, keeping a journal between sessions helps stimulate the work in progress when the group is not together. At support-group meetings, time should be set aside for people to read aloud from their journals, if they choose. These readings are a further step in trying on, or testing out, the comfort of an idea, while using the dynamics of the gathered listeners to induce the flow of new thoughts and feelings. Reading from journals should be received with attentive listening, and without comment. The reading, like the writing, is personal for the journal keeper and provides him with the chance to appreciate and benefit from his work.

Additional reading about keeping a journal:

Baldwin, Christina. *One to One: Self-Understanding through Journal Writing.* New York: M. Evans & Co., Inc., 1977.

Progoff, Ira. *At a Journal Workshop: The Basic Text and Guide for Using the Intensive Journal.* New York: Dialogue House Library, 1975.

The use of an egalitarian process in any group affirms its members by establishing and protecting certain major priorities; namely, the inclusion (as providers of resources), the valuing, and the nurturing of every member of the group. The affirming process is a necessity in a group that hopes to provide individuals with support: it should reflect the group's commitment to encourage and reinforce each member to develop his skills and self-esteem, by sharing the responsibility for the direction and running of the group equally, and by making sure that the ground rules and decisions are established by the group as a whole. Even though not every parent will choose to join a formalized parent support group, still all families, clubs, and religious and community groups

Group Process

can be viewed and cultivated as certain alternative types of support groups. The following guidelines for group process are thus applicable and equally valuable for facilitating the work done in any support-giving group.

Meeting Facilitation

THE ROLE OF THE FACILITATOR: WHAT IT IS AND WHAT IT ISN'T

Facilitators are the group members who help the group accomplish what it wants to do. The facilitators plan an agenda, and at each meeting, after making sure that the agenda suits the group, the facilitators lead them through the planned activities. While others are concentrating on the activity at hand—sharing, journaling, brainstorming—the facilitators are doing the same but are also thinking about how the group is functioning (Can we finish this discussion in another four minutes, or should we contract for more time?) Orchestrating all of these things is a skill that can be learned, given experienced models, accurate information, and practice. The facilitators are responsible *to* the group as the persons chosen to carry out the group's purposes. They make no deci-

The section "Meeting Facilitation" in this chapter was written by Anne Toensmeier.

sions for the group. They prepare agendas, activities, and plans, but these are merely suggestions: the group must authorize each plan, each change. A facilitator needs to be flexible enough to scrap her well-laid plans if the group has other wishes. In addition, she is not expected to be the expert on parenting or a perfect parent, and it isn't necessary that she be up-to-date on all the current parenting manuals. She is not an authority, a guard, or a rescuer, whose duty is to solve the problems of group members.

Another part of the role of facilitator is sharing the responsibility with cofacilitators and apprentices. While a facilitator can lead a group by herself, we find that two are better than one. Cofacilitators can ease the pressure for each other. By taking turns at running different parts of the agenda, they give each other chances for mental preparation, they support each other, and they get a better sense of the "vibes" in the room. While one facilitator leads an activity, the other can act as timekeeper or scribe, as well as keeping her eyes and ears open. After the meeting, during their own evaluation, cofacilitators can check their perceptions with each other.

A facilitator who has called together a group because of her own needs may wish that she could plan an agenda that would help her with her own personal problems. If her children are teen-agers, while many group members have preschool children, she cannot expect the topics to be limited to drugs and dating. While the facilitator's needs, and those of every individual, must be considered, the fact is that *the needs of the group must come first.* Our hypothetical leader with teen-age children may have to set aside her desire for parent-of-adolescent topics for a while. (Perhaps she could agree on "Coping with Children's Defiance" or "Letting Them Go.") A facilitator also should make sure that other members' needs do not outweigh those of the whole group. Actually, the group is more than the sum of its members, and it may evolve into something that is different from anything its individual members intended.

While every group, and every facilitator's style, is unique, the facilitators must try to set a tone that is positive, caring, open, encouraging, and not too serious. The assumption is that every member present can grow, find support, discover her own answers, and offer much to the group. Without a trace of sarcasm or put-down, there can be humor and lightness.

In order to maintain the positive tone and safe atmosphere of a group, it is wise to ask for agreement on a few ground rules. Some are negotiable; some are not. The rules that are essential are these:

- Everyone has the right to pass. Choosing not to join an activity or discussion is not viewed as a negative judgment of the activity, facilitator, or group, but as an assertion of one's right to step back when that seems right.
- There are no wrong answers. People's views should be respected as they are expressed, without challenge, judgment, rebuttal, or probing questions (Clarification can be requested, but digging for information is out.).
- Focus on the positives in people and affirm them. The only unwelcome comments are put-downs.

In addition, a group may want to make its own ground rules in answer to questions like these:

- Does the group welcome visitors?
- Does it welcome new members?

A group might have special needs that require ground rules:

- In a discussion, no one speaks a second time until everyone has a first turn.

THE PROCESS OF FACILITATION[1]

The first step in facilitating is planning a tentative, timed agenda. This proposed agenda is tentative until the group approves it; it is timed—that is, approximate times are assigned to each activity—to ensure that:

- the agenda can be accomplished in the assigned meeting time.

---

[1] Berit Lakey. *No Magic Meetings* (Philadelphia, Pa.: New Society Press, 1980).

- the group doesn't get bogged down on a minor point without ever getting to the major one.
- the meeting ends when people expect it to.
- different items on the agenda get the right proportion of attention.
- activities that should go swiftly, such as brainstorming or quick sharing in pairs, do so.
- the group be responsible about time.

It is important that the group know roughly how much time is assigned to each activity, and that it agree on the time allotted. If an item turns out to take longer than expected, a facilitator asks the group what it wants to do:

"We have only five minutes left for our discussion of television, and I sense that people have lots more to say. Shall we stop in five minutes, or would you like to take another fifteen? If we take fifteen minutes more, shall we eliminate today's book review, or shall we close fifteen minutes late?" When group members are part of such a decision, they are not likely to feel resentful about a meeting that ends fifteen minutes past schedule or, on the other hand, about not getting their say.

Another factor to consider in planning an agenda is the dynamics of *sharing* and the effect of participation in large and small groups. It is good to have some of both at each meeting. In groups of two or three, people may feel safer exploring ideas and sharing feelings, and less self-conscious about the value of their contribution. In the larger group people can contribute some of what they have shared in twos or threes, can benefit from a wider range of experience, and can get a sense of the whole group as an entity. If the meeting is quite large, as in an intergenerational gathering, it is necessary to have small groups in order for everyone to be heard.

After considering the time allotments and the dynamics of the group and possible activities, the facilitators make up an agenda. Here is a sample of an agenda for a session on television and the family:

1. "Goods and News"	5 minutes
2. Agenda review	5 minutes
3. Sharing, in pairs: "One thing I like about TV"	2 minutes each way
4. Individual (silent) reading of articles about TV's effects on children	10 minutes
5. Report and review on articles (in the group)	15 minutes
6. Quick break: Musical Laps[2]	3 minutes
7. Discussion: "How TV affects my family"	20 minutes
8. Brainstorm: "I Wish . . ." personal statements about TV	5 minutes
9. Announcements	5 minutes
10. Evaluation of meeting	5 minutes
11. Closing: Each person states one TV goal for this week	5 minutes

In any meeting, the first item on the agenda is some sort of brief (five- to ten-minute) *gathering process*. There are several reasons for a gathering exercise:

- to acknowledge and pay attention, however briefly, to each person present.
- to help each person turn her attention away from the chaos she has left behind (clinging children as she left home, piles of papers to correct, car troubles on the way) and give attention to what is happening here and now.
- to set the tone of positiveness.
- to acknowledge that each person brings to this time a new assortment of experiences, feelings, and concerns.
- to give people a chance to tell whatever is so much on their minds that it's going to come out during the meeting sooner or later, anyway.

A gathering exercise is planned to focus on positive things. For some people, it will be very difficult to find something positive to share. The facilitator encourages such people, but without pushing

---

[2] See page 155.

—they have a right to pass. The most common gathering exercise is excitement sharing, also known as "goods and news." Everyone who wants to participate tells briefly about some excitement, however small, in her life or her day. If the exercise is new to members, a facilitator might introduce it by going first: "My excitement was getting two letters from friends in the mail today." A variation might be having everyone tell about what she had for breakfast or what sign of spring she saw. Many group members come to cherish excitement sharing and to look forward to it.

Sometimes it might seem wise to share "not-so-goods," as well as "goods." In this case, the facilitators must use discretion. It is important to accept people's situations, and if someone has barely escaped a car accident on the way to the meeting, she needs to tell about it; the gathering exercise, however, should prepare people to think clearly and positively. If this is a first meeting or if a new person is attending, the gathering process will include introductions. If someone comes in breathlessly, later in the meeting, at the soonest convenience a facilitator should ask if she has an excitement to share; this greets the latecomer, includes her, and helps her, too, to focus on the present.

Another item early in the agenda is always the *agenda review*. Because the facilitator's job is to help the group decide on and carry out what it wants to do, it is important to check early to make sure that the proposed agenda meets the group's needs. After the facilitators have written the proposed agenda—complete with proposed times for each activity—on a large sheet of newsprint or shelf paper, it should be taped to the wall so that everyone can see the plan and the changes as they occur.

After a facilitator has explained the agenda, she asks the group if it suits them. She makes sure to get a clear answer of one kind or another—nods and yeses if the answer is positive, not just the glazed look of a group member who feels she has no say. If the group as a whole wants to make changes, she records those changes for all to see. Later in the meeting, if people begin following tangents or taking more time than was budgeted, she reminds them of the agenda they've agreed on and asks them to make a conscious choice about any change in time or topic.

In planning the "body" of the meeting—what happens between the agenda review and the announcements, evaluation, and closing—the facilitators can draw on a great variety of activities and processes, and they must use their best judgment about how to order activities. It is preferable for group members to start with comfortable activities and move on to more challenging ones—sharing a light topic before sharing heavier feelings and memories; sharing in twos before sharing with the whole group. Some groups are never going to feel comfortable with certain activities at all, so in these cases the facilitators should choose less threatening forms. The purpose of the group meeting, rather than forcing unwilling participation, is to help each member find support while she grows in her own way.

In general, when planning a meeting and the discussion of a given topic, the facilitators should try to keep the approach positive, fresh, and creative. If the topic is to be anger, instead of sharing only some experiences such as "a time when I was furious at my child," people might focus as well on "a time when I handled my anger well." They might also brainstorm outlets for angry parents, keeping their ideas light, if not silly—"pound a Swiss steak, yell nonsense words, shake out all your throw rugs whether they're dirty or not." Working from a positive attitude—rather than dragging the whole group down in feelings of hopelessness and despair, for instance—frees enough available energy and attention to meet the negatives when they come up. If a topic presents a real problem for one member, the group can give him some special time for attentive listening and, if it seems appropriate, offer group problem solving (on the spot only if it is an emergency, otherwise at another specially planned meeting, if all agree).

The members who plan the agenda may also want to rely on what they know, and can guess, about people's physical and emotional highs and lows: people need a change of pace or two in the course of a meeting. Facilitators should watch for "energy sag"—and it seems to come after sustained hard thinking or sitting. One way to raise energy levels is to make sure that no one activity lasts very long. For example, a group can approach a topic through different activities. Fantasies, group discussion, and reading from journals might use different mental, if not physical, muscles.

Another choice is to interrupt the topic with a change-of-pace activity like a game, a song, or a stretch. Ideally, it will raise the energy level, circulate the blood, wake up sleeping muscles, and release some laughter without dispersing the group for half an hour. While a plain old break may seem the best choice, it invariably takes too long and dissipates people's energy and attention. Cooperative games are an excellent pace changer for people who are comfortable with them. In intergenerational and teachers' groups, in which people are more willing to play "for the children's sake," they go well—but many adults have so much embarrassment and discomfort that games may be counterproductive. Changing places, stretches, songs, or the old stand-by quick refreshments can help. A quick crafts project, such as making a card for an absent member, is another possibility. The facilitators can change the agenda and introduce change-of-pace activities whenever feasible. It is also completely appropriate to interrupt the plans and be open to suggestions. Rarely will anyone object.

Although the emphasis in groups is on encouraging people to discover their own answers and values, it is appropriate, as a starting point, for the facilitators to present some theory central to the meeting's topic—affirmation, feelings, communication skills, for example. Giving a *book review* on the topic might also help to introduce discussion. The facilitators should present the theory briefly, clearly, and undogmatically. It is important to stick to the time limit, so that everyone may have a chance to participate.

There are certain techniques that a facilitator may use during a meeting to start up, and keep, the momentum going:

BRAINSTORMING: As quickly as possible, members of the group call out ideas (even farfetched ones), which pertain to the topic, while someone jots them down on large newsprint. This activity lasts no more than five minutes. Nobody comments on the ideas.

SETTING PRIORITIES: This activity is especially valuable during the agenda review. The facilitator helps the group decide which topics it wants to deal with first, which second, and so forth. The facilitator may take a straw vote, in which everyone can vote several times, and the votes for each item are then tallied. The straw vote, an informal vote for getting the sense of people's preferences, can be used on other occasions. Making major decisions, however, is done by consensus.

REHEARSAL TIME: After explaining the activity that is to follow, the facilitator gives everyone two minutes for silent preparation or reflection.

THINK AND LISTEN: After a few minutes of thinking, everyone who wants to shares, one by one, her thinking on the given topic, while everyone else listens, but no one comments. A strict time limit, perhaps two minutes apiece, is observed. This exercise eliminates argument and encourages the sharing of thoughts and fresh approaches.

ATTENTIVE LISTENING: Everyone listens carefully to each speaker without interruption; if the meaning is complicated or unclear, the facilitator might restate what she thinks she hears, checking her perception for accuracy. There may be an understanding that people can ask only *clarifying questions* ("Then, are you saying that . . . ?" or "Does this mean that . . . ?").

DISCUSSION: While people engage in exchanging ideas, the facilitator remains sensitive to keeping time, staying on the subject, and giving opportunities for everyone to talk. In groups in which a few people dominate discussions, there might be a ground rule that no one speaks a second time until everyone who wishes to has spoken once.

UNFINISHED BUSINESS: When a dialogue has gone on for a while and is occupying the attention of only two or three people, a facilitator suggests that it is unfinished business, and that the interested people are to finish the dialogue at some time other than during the meeting. This request keeps the group's energy high and yet meets everyone's needs.

CONSENSUS: When the group needs to make a decision, everyone must agree to it. If no consensus can be reached, the group leaves the decision for a later time. Sometimes a group reaches consensus only after a member or some members have graciously given in, but only by their own choice. The facilitators try to get the sense of the meeting; they may want to check out their perceptions by expressing them to the group: "My sense is that everyone would be comfortable with a ground rule of no smoking at meetings. Am I correct?"

Once the main work of the meeting is over, it is time for announcements, evaluation, and closing. *Announcements* may include such housekeeping arrangements as when and where the group meets next, and who will be responsible for book reviews or refreshments.

Evaluation is an important part of each meeting. It is another way for members to have a say in how the group functions, and it gives facilitators information about what is working and what needs to be changed. The person running the evaluation—this is a good place for apprentices to start out—divides a large sheet of paper vertically with a line. One side has a plus sign, the other an upward-pointing arrow; these stand for "What's been good?" and "What needs to be changed?" Starting with the positive, since negatives can become habitual and are discouraging, the group brainstorms items for each. Positives need not be profound: the carrot cake may have made the evening for everyone; it need not have been so for everyone, either. As in brainstorming, the facilitators accept and record any suggestion without response. The same process is used for the "need to be changed" items with emphasis on how those changes might be effected. The pace is quick. Evaluation takes about five minutes.

Instead of letting people drift away after the evaluation, the *closing circle* draws everyone together for a moment. Spending the last few minutes considering each other, not a topic, affirms everyone. It also ends the meeting definitely and on a positive note. Often the exercise chosen might be sharing, around the circle:

- something you're looking forward to.
- your favorite thing to do on a snowy day.
- a single word that stood out at the meeting.

Or it may be a quick activity, like "Umaah!" Everyone holds hands, crouching very close, and slowly, getting louder and louder, as they move their hands upward, says, "UmmmAAHH!" Another choice might be a song. The predecessor of all our support groups eventually adopted as a theme song a jovial round called "Aurora." For groups who enjoy it, a group hug can't be beat.

THE FACILITATOR AS TROUBLE-SHOOTER

Special problems inevitably come up in support groups just as they do in families. When people are considering values, especially about their children, when they are developing relationships beyond the intellectual with each other, especially when they are seeking answers and considering changes in their lives, conflicts do arise. A support group that runs too smoothly might be suspect. Conflict, we remind ourselves with clenched teeth, is not something to avoid. If dealt with openly, it is healthy. The facilitators can prevent conflict from becoming troublesome by thoughtful planning, strictly observed ground rules, directness, positiveness, and sensitivity.

One conflict, arising from dashed expectations, that may be felt by many newcomers to support groups is that they do not get the answers that they desperately crave. They may seize the lapels of the facilitator, asking "What *do* you do about punishment, then?" "Shall I let my child play with guns?" The answer—that there's no one "right" response, that each of us is her own best judge—leaves them frustrated. This happened to me years ago when I first came in contact with the Nonviolence and Children Program. After the evening program I felt so unsatisfied that I asked the facilitator to talk with me privately. We went into the empty kitchen of the conference center, and I said, "Look. All of that was very nice, but I have an eighteen-month-old child at home, I'm pregnant, and I've got to know—shall I spank or not?" She said all of the things to me that I now know to be true, about how all of the good things that happened between me and my child were what mattered, and I thanked her politely, but I knew that I still didn't have an answer. Such a feeling of urgency may well prevent an individual from giving attention to what's happening in the group. It may interfere with the process of the whole group, too. The facilitators must try to address the urgently felt need without sacrificing the needs of the group.

How does the facilitator respond to the person with the urgent question? Here are some approaches:

- Explain why building a sense of community within the group and gaining understanding of her own childhood must both come before the questioner can come up with her own answer.
- Encourage her: "Your question is so important that we should give it some extra consideration. Let's plan a session so we can deal with this in depth."
- Continue: "But in the meantime, I would like you to do some research [or thinking or observation], and I will find you some resources."
- Assign her a special project, such as assembling readings on the question that plagues her, to be used in a macrosession (at which the group would attempt to provide support by reading and responding to the material).
- Ask her to do a journal segment on the subject that is so pressing. At the next meeting, she may read her entry aloud, without comment or responses from the group, if she chooses. Such an opportunity would allow her to present her viewpoint without needing to defend it.
- Give everyone a "puzzling question" to take home. It might be this: "How does the issue that's most burning for you right now relate to affirmation?" At the next meeting, each person has three to five minutes to share the results of her inquiry. Considering her problem in the light of affirmation may put a new perspective on it.

- At the beginning of each meeting set aside a "focus time," when anyone can request a specified period of time, perhaps five or ten minutes, with the full attention of the group, to state her problem, indicating whether she wants a response. If she does want suggestions, she might decide to listen to them without responding to them. Someone else might take notes on the suggestions. If she does decide to respond to the suggestions, it might be in Goal Wish form: "The two most interesting ideas to me are . . . and . . . . The doubt I have is. . . ."

There are other common problems that support groups fall prey to. Unless they are attentive, the group might list toward complaint, commiseration, or the encounter mode on the one hand, or mere intellectualization on the other. They may become passive, allowing the facilitators or one of the members to do all the thinking or talking. They may play it too safe, failing to try new topics or activities when the old ones have become comfortable. They may enjoy each other so much that somehow they never get through an agenda. The group may lose members by attrition, dwindling to a core of old faithfuls. Fortunately, leaders have some good tools for working on these problems:

- good planning that makes sure that people get adequate time for working on their own personal problems (by sharing or journaling). Such support keeps the seminar from becoming an intellectual exercise.
- clearly stated expectations to which everyone has agreed.
- ground rules to prevent encounter approaches, negativity, commiseration, patronizing, lack of choice.
- evaluations that give members both input and constructive outlets for their dissatisfaction.
- clear, direct questions: "John, are Mike's comments hard for you to listen to right now?" "Rachel, you look frustrated. Do you feel that you were heard?" "Does anyone who hasn't spoken already want to say something?"
- positive action, when necessary, to reverse a negative situation: "I think we're all feeling hopeless. How can we turn this around?" "Wendy, you certainly must have had quite a week. But was there something positive that you could share?" "We're all feeling discouraged about our parenting. Let's

spend a moment appreciating some good bit of parenting we've done recently."

The facilitator's job can make one feel like a tightrope walker. Avoiding common pitfalls takes an especially good sense of balance. After the group has defined what it wants to do, the leaders have a certain responsibility to keep the balance. Actually, though, the leaders are not so totally responsible. As group members become more experienced by following and practicing an effective process, as they come to feel encouraged and affirmed, they will take on more and more responsibility for achieving balance through mutual support.

Additional reading about group process:

Jervis, Kathe. "Teachers Learning from Teachers." *Learning*, August/September 1978, pp. 68–70, 74.

Lakey, Berit. *No Magic Meetings*. Philadelphia, Pa.: New Society Press, 1980.

Rogers, Carl. "Personal Power at Work," *Psychology Today*, April 1977, 10:60–62, 93–94.

Intergenerational Workshops

Intergenerational workshops, as developed by the Nonviolence and Children Program, have four goals. As with all our work, our primary goal is to have fun, to celebrate and affirm with others our joy in life and living. Secondly, these sessions are aimed at the development of communication between people of differing ages. Thirdly, insights are gleaned as to the resources of various age groups and individuals. Lastly, workshops provide an experience that will assist people in feeling more confident, comfortable, and capable in pursuing intergenerational relationships in their own lives.

The agendas followed in intergenerational workshops do not differ greatly from the other models used by the Nonviolence and Children Program, as described in the previous section on Meeting Facilitation. As with any workshop, a safe atmosphere is created through the use of ground rules for the duration of the session. All exercises and activities are planned to build a sense of community within the group and to heighten the degree of trust felt between individuals and the whole. There may be individual activities, talking in twos or threes, small group projects, or whole group discussions. Emphasis is on having fun together, while getting to know others. Games, dramatization, discussion, music, art, dancing, are all utilized for intellectual, physical, and emotional stimulation. Time is set aside for focusing on individuals' responses to all these activities. What do you feel when you dance the Virginia reel with someone half your size? Are there surprises when you share experiences with someone three times your age? Insights can be simple, astounding, and reassuring, all at the same time.

There are a few specifics that apply particularly to sessions that go across several generations:

- If at all possible, use group members of varying ages to plan and facilitate the sessions. Use resources that are "natural" or integral to the group—a piano player, or song writer, a game

known to young people that could be taught by them to the whole group.

- Activities that are considered "low-risk," that foster a sense of trust within the gathering, should set the tone at the outset, even if the group has had experience in this kind of session before.
- Vary the pace of activities to account for attention spans and disabilities. A time of quiet sharing could be followed by a game or physical task. Offer alternative activities at times, to give some participants more time to relax or feel comfortable.
- The trust level should be quite high before any child-directed or especially active projects are introduced.
- Include some discussion after most exercises, and listen for comments that might give insights into attitudes or the level of trust in the community. Be prepared to record these comments, and possibly discuss them at some point in the workshop.
- Don't cast the agenda in bronze! View it as a plan that gives structure to a session, but that is still flexible enough to respond to the group's needs as they emerge before and during the session.
- Utilize tangible items—drawings, charts, banners, valentines— to evaluate and mark the group's experiences of the session. Plan to leave these with the group or return them to the individuals after the evaluation.

The following activities have worked well in intergenerational-workshop settings and are listed in order of "risk," or projected willingness to participate:

- cooperative games.
- group tasks: treasure hunts, scavenger lists, building projects.
- sharing, in pairs, of common experiences: one's favorite pastime at five years of age.
- sharing about discoveries in nature, or about personal treasures or keepsakes, with small or large groups.
- drawing: individual or group projects.
- creating "sculpture" by group members posing together to represent a theme such as a forest or a waterfall.
- mirroring exercises in pairs of differing sizes (see p. 158).

- role playing, dramatizations, especially when reversing roles.
- quiet time together: reading, walking, etc.
- trust walks (see pp. 46, 156).
- child-taught activities: children lead the group in learning games, songs, etc.
- affirmation exercises: making hand and body silhouettes (pp. 15, 153–54), valentines (pp. 151–52), a group banner; having a group celebration.

T oo often we react to or think about an issue over and over from the same viewpoint, or without realizing that we bring to the issue a particular bias, that leads us back to a frustrating, no-progress response. The exercises included here are intended to spark fresh reasoning, to make us look at particular issues from new angles. In each exercise there is an emphasis on affirming oneself and others. The purpose is not to compel a Pollyanna attitude, but to encourage reaching for and building on positive elements rather than negative ones. The exercises can be collected and kept for future review and redone at various intervals, in order to chart changing views and growing skills. When used as group tools, the written exercises, first worked on individually, can then be shared with partners or the whole group, with the protection of ground rules that make it clear that there are no right or wrong answers, only different points of view.

Exercises and Clarifying Tools

Wherever possible we have attempted to trace the origin of, and give proper credit for, all "borrowed" exercises and strategies included in this book, but as this sort of material is part of a great new flush in self-help and education tools, many ideas have been passed along like folk tales, altered and enhanced as they go, no longer directly attributable to a specific originator. To any and all of those unnamed contributors who have added to the information resources reflected here, we say a warm thank you.

Affirmation

VALENTINES

Our daily lives would be enriched if we could include some of the joy and celebration of special holidays. Valentines are wonderful to send and receive all year round.

INDIVIDUALLY:

1. Think of something you could use some more appreciation for. Write yourself a telegram of congratulations: "Great

job, Bob Jones! You fold wash like a professional!" Hang it on the refrigerator door for all to see.

2. Choose one fine quality that really shines through these days, write it in big letters on a piece of paper, and tape it to your mirror so that you can see yourself as you really are: patient, cheerful, etc.

3. For your journal: Describe a time when you felt especially good about yourself, a time when you handled a situation well. What special qualities in yourself did you draw on? Did others recognize your achievement? How did they show it? How do you feel about that time or incident now?

IN THE FAMILY:

1. Write a little love note, thank-you note, or a few words of encouragement to someone in the family, and tuck it in a lunch bag, pin it to a pillow, or tape it to a mirror.

2. At a family meeting discuss affirmation. Ask for examples of put-downs and put-ups. Provide art materials (paper, crayons, old magazines, scissors, and glue), and have a valentine party. Write family members' names on slips of paper, and have each person pick one. Each person creates a valentine that shows some special things about the person who is to receive it (interests, strengths, successes, admired qualities). After about twenty minutes of work, take turns presenting the creations, telling your valentine and the group why it is especially for that person.

IN THE CLASSROOM:

1. Discuss affirmation. Ask for examples of put-downs. Brainstorm ways to affirm others, and ways to affirm ourselves.

2. Give each child a piece of paper, with the outline of a T-shirt on it (better yet, have each child bring in a real T-shirt to decorate, using any washable textile crayons). Have each design a motif that is about him: something he is proud of or is known for, or that he dreams to do or have. Hang the shirts around the room. One class made real shirts, wore them to an assembly, and sang a made-up song called "I Love my Shirt!"

3. Make an envelope with each child's name on it, and tack the envelopes up on the bulletin board. Tell the class that these envelopes are mailboxes for happy thoughts. When the chil-

dren see someone else having success, doing something difficult, acting especially kind, or just being their usual delightful self, have them write a little note of appreciation and put it in the person's envelope.

4. If a child is out sick for a few days, have each classmate write one sentence on a strip of paper, telling something she likes or enjoys about her absent friend. Fold up the strips of paper and put them in an envelope or plastic bottle, to be sent home as get-well medicine.

5. Have the children begin a journal. Each day before class ends have them record a success, or "I'm proud of . . . ," statement.

IN THE SUPPORT GROUP:

1. Ask each group member to think of the person in his family whom he gives the least affirmation to. Write a brief note, appreciating that person. Ask for one or two volunteers to read their note. The affirmations should be sent, if possible, or kept in the members' journals.

2. Brainstorm the kinds of things that keep us from giving "valentines" more often (awkwardness? fear? thoughtlessness?).

3. Take ten or fifteen minutes for the group members to make a valentine to take home to their families.

4. Before closing, take turns around the circle, and have each member turn to the person on her left and give her a spoken valentine: "Mary, one thing I appreciate about you is. . . ."

AFFIRMATION SILHOUETTES

The most noticeable outward sign of our individual uniqueness is our physical appearance. Silhouettes—outline tracings—of our body, hands, or head make a personalized, one-of-a-kind background for written affirmations. Choosing the size of the silhouettes will depend on the time and materials available and on the number of people in the group. Whichever size your group chooses, be sure to do one for every member. Before adding affirmations to the sheets, talk about put-downs and put-ups. Explain affirmation and how it helps people grow. Ask for examples of times when people were put down or affirmed.

HAND SILHOUETTES

Each person traces the outline of one hand on a standard sheet of paper and writes her name on the hand. Group members move around the room, writing brief affirmations on each sheet.

HEAD SILHOUETTES

Tape a large sheet of paper on a wall or blackboard. Focus a spotlight or high-intensity light onto the paper. Position a person between the paper and light, so that a distinct shadow is cast on the paper. Trace the shadow with a felt-tip pen. Have group members write special appreciations on the paper around the tracing.

The Art of Giving and Receiving Support

SUPPORT LIFE LINE [1]

1. Draw a line to represent your life span. At the left of the line mark the year of your birth. The right end of the line represents your death. Use a dot to mark where you think you are now in that span.

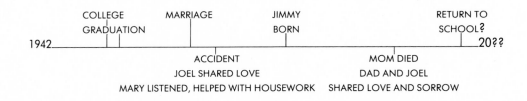

2. Using dots above the line, mark important high points in your life. Note what those occasions were and who shared them with you.

3. Beneath the line, note the low points in your life, and indicate who supported you through those times. What type of support did they give?

[1] Adapted from Sidney B. Simon, Leland W. Howe, and Howard Kirschenbaum, "Life Line," in *Values Clarification* (New York: Hart Publishing Co,. 1972), pp. 304–5.

EXERCISES AND CLARIFYING TOOLS

4. Mark some highs and lows you project in your future. Who might you expect to rely on or share those times with?

HELP WANTED/HELP AVAILABLE

1. Write an imaginary advertisement for your local paper. Describe your talents as a support giver. List what you feel you can offer. What do you require in exchange?

2. Write another ad seeking the support you would most like to receive right now in your life.

GROUP GAMES:

MUSICAL LAPS[2]

The group gradually forms a circle, all facing the back of the person ahead, close together, each with hands on the waist of

---

[2] We learned this game from Sandra Cangiano at a faculty workshop at Abington Friends School, Abington, Pennsylvania.

the person ahead. One person begins to sing and everyone walks forward. When the singing stops, everyone sits down in the lap of person behind him. If the whole group succeeds in sitting in laps without anyone falling to the floor, the group wins. If people fall down, gravity wins, and the group tries again.

Discuss how cooperation and competition affect giving and getting support.

TRUST WALK [3]

Have group members form pairs. If there are varied ages in the group, pair off older with younger. One partner in each pair chooses to be the leader first. The second partner is blindfolded or closes her eyes tightly and allows herself to be led around a prescribed area. The lead partner holds his partner's hand and stays physically close while leading her carefully. During the first two minutes of the walk, verbal directions may be given. During the second two minutes the guiding should be done silently. After four minutes have the partners switch roles. The lead partner is responsible for the safety of the blind partner. The lead partner can enrich the blind partner's experience by helping the person discover textures and objects in the environment.

Discuss how support was given and trust built. What felt good about the role of the support person, the trust person? Which role did people like better? What new or special feelings did people have about their partners after the walk?

Talking it Out

STORIES WE TELL

One way we share insights is through relating stories about our past. The stories we tell are a means of conveying our experiential learning.

---

[3] Robert C. Hawley and Isabel L. Hawley, "Observation Walk," in *Developing Human Potential: A Handbook of Activities for Personal and Social Growth* (Amherst, Mass; ERA Press, 1975), p. 44. See also p. 46.

INDIVIDUALLY:

In your journal write down a story that one of your parents has told you. Write it in the first person, just as they might tell it. What do you think is the message of this story? Is there a story that you would like to tell your parents, to explain or illustrate a point? If so, write it in your journal. What is the moral of your story? Consider telling the story or the point to your parents, if that is possible.

IN THE FAMILY:

Ask family members to remember special adventures shared by the group. Have them pick one that everyone remembers well. Choose a scribe who will record the story while family members dictate a description of the event. This exercise could be repeated at other meetings, so that the family could compile a series of family adventures. Grandparents and other relatives could be invited to contribute to the storytelling and recording. Be sure to include time for observations, summing up, and sharing insights.

IN THE CLASSROOM:

Break the class into groups of four or six. Have a brief sharing time in which students have a few minutes each to relate "Stories My Parents Always Tell." Have each group choose one story they all like or can relate to, and, given five minutes' preparation, present an improvised skit telling the story. Each group must treat its story as if it "belongs" to them, presenting it with the same respect and feeling that the elders deliver it with. The skits could be presented in mime, allowing the other class members to guess the story. After all the skits are given, discuss common themes that appear. Why do parents tell stories of their past? Do the stories change with the generations? What will be the special themes of this class's future stories?

IN THE SUPPORT GROUP:

In pairs tell briefly a story your parents used to tell you when you were growing up. How did you react to it? Next tell a story that would be important to you to tell your children. In the large group discuss the benefits of storytelling. How can it go awry?

Mirroring[4]

Communication involves more than just words. Mirroring is a technique that uses only body language to demonstrate how we can communicate without words. Group members pair off and stand facing each other, leaving room for movement between the pairs. One partner is the leader, and the other is a mirror. On a signal from the facilitator, the lead partners slowly begin to move in place, raising arms or legs, swaying, bending, or twisting. The mirror must follow the movements of the leader exactly. The goal is to communicate well enough so that there can be a complete duplication of the information sent by the leader. This draws on the concentration, observation, intuition, and sensitivity of both partners. After three minutes, the partners exchange roles. After another three minutes both partners are leaders/mirrors simultaneously, concentrating on developing motions cooperatively. When the mirroring is completed, the group discusses the feelings they had during the different phases of the exercise.

SINGING WITH FEELING

Choose any simple and well-known tune like "Row, Row, Row Your Boat" and see how it sounds when sung with different feelings. After singing it through once or twice, group members suggest a feeling —angry, scared, proud, etc.—and the group sings the song in the tone of voice requested.

Understanding and Accepting Our Feelings

INDIVIDUALLY:

1. In your journal keep a random log of your feelings for a period of about a week. In each entry briefly note the day, the time, what is happening, and the feeling that is coloring that moment. For example:

---

[4] Robert C. Hawley and Isabel L. Hawley, "Mirroring Sequence," in *Developing Human Potential: A Handbook of Activities for Personal and Social Growth* (Amherst, Mass., ERA Press, 1975), pp. 50–51.

Monday, 8:15 A.M.: Everyone has gone for the day . . . except me. Even the dog has gone off for a nap. It is sunny and brisk outside. I've just made a cup of tea, and I'm ready to get to work. I feel determined, positive, ready to go.

Tuesday, 2:45 P.M.: The mail just arrived . . . more bills! I have to be at the school to watch the boys' soccer game, and I'm relieved to have an excuse to get out in the fresh air. I'm fighting discouragement.

Do not analyze or judge the feelings; just let them take form. Name your responses as accurately as you can. Don't just stick to words like "happy," "sad," or "angry." Reach for a broader, more definitive vocabulary.

2. Review the log and see if there is a feeling that seems central or one that keeps turning up. Write a dialogue, as if you were talking with the feeling: begin by profiling the feeling and listing its appearances during the week. The "conversation" might run like this:

DISCOURAGEMENT:
1. You showed up on Tuesday afternoon, with the arrival of the bills.
2. You disappeared once I got to the soccer field.
3. You returned Wednesday morning after everyone raced out of the house late, with the house in a shambles.
4. Wednesday night you permeated the house. Everyone was complaining and I just wanted to lock myself in the bathroom, but it was too grubby.
5. Thursday you prowled around in my head all day, but I worked like crazy and refused to pay attention to you.
6. Today I sense that you are lurking somewhere nearby, waiting for a tired moment when you will confront me.

Now address the feeling. Let it speak to you from its own character. Tell it what you feel about it.

DISCOURAGEMENT: "I am here, waiting. I will not go away until you face me."

CAROLINE: "I don't need you. I am ignoring you. I won't let you drag me down."

DISCOURAGEMENT: "But I have things to show you. I'm full of worries and fears that you ought to pay attention to."

Let the dialogue take its own course. Do not guide it or try to get rid of the feelings that arise. The goal of this exercise is to get to know and express your feelings.

IN THE FAMILY OR THE CLASSROOM:

1. Read a children's book about feelings to the group. Let the readers in the group take turns reading out loud. Use the story as a starting point for discussing feelings. A book like *My Momma Says There Aren't Any Zombies, Ghosts, Vampires, Creatures, Demons, Monsters, Fiends, Goblins, or Things,* by Judith Viorst is a delightful way to start a discussion about scary feelings. It could stimulate a great story-swapping session about fearful and fun-filled times. *The Terrible Thing That Happened at Our House,* by Marge Blaine, could bring out feelings about Mother going to work. *The Tenth Good Thing about Barney,* also by Judith Viorst, could open some discussion that might relieve fears and anxieties about death.

2. Have a puppet play to act out some situations that portray feelings. You might begin by performing part of the story from one of the books the group has read; then have groups of two or three improvise stories about "A Happy Day," "A Terrible Scare," etc.

3. Draw up a Feelings Vocabulary List. Begin with the headings: Happiness, Unhappiness, Anger, Fear, Like, Dislike, Discomfort, and Concern; then list as many variations and intensities as possible under each concept. Post a sheet of paper for each term, and make the lists accessible so that everyone can see them. Add other headings as they seem appropriate. You can also do this exercise individually, keeping the list in your journal and adding to it as your awareness and your emotional vocabulary grow.

4. Play the Feelings Alphabet Game. Taking turns around the circle, each player names a feeling beginning with the consecutive letters of the alphabet: A is for aggravated, B is for blissful, C is for crabby. The game becomes more fun when appropriate faces and body gestures accompany the words. For the letters that are harder to fill in, let players make up a word, and describe not only what it means but when one might feel that way. For instance, X is for xabulated; that means you feel as if you've been done in: "I feel xabulated

when I have been standing in the grocery line for ten minutes, and just when it's my turn they close the line to change the register tape."

IN THE SUPPORT GROUP:

1. To elicit feelings in a session, have members share, in pairs: "The happiest time in the year for me." Then share: "A time when I get depressed." In the full group, brainstorm: "What I do when I'm happy"; then, "What I do to get over being depressed."

2. Share success stories: "Something I'm afraid to do, but do, anyway"; "A time I got angry enough to stand up for myself," etc.

3. Offer "focus time" in the group. At the beginning of each meeting ask if anyone would like five or ten minutes of focus time to verbalize, discuss, or otherwise deal with feelings. During this time the person has an opportunity to express himself, while receiving the supportive awareness of the group.

   For instance, Beverly has decided to run for political office for the first time. She might request five minutes' focus time to let out some of her anxiety about giving speeches. The person sitting on either side of her might hold her hand, someone might put an arm around her, or she might ask that the whole group arrange itself in front of her as an audience while she expresses her fear.

   "Oh, boy, do I love being the center of attention!" She might laugh, adding mockingly, "And I know the whole world is just dying to hear what I have to say." Perhaps she will cry and say, "I'm so scared. I'm afraid I'll make a blunder in front of everyone."

   In the warm attention of the group she can confront her anxiety. When the allotted time has ended, the facilitator or other group members can help Beverly refocus on the group by asking her upbeat or trivia questions that bring her thinking and feelings back to the present time and circumstances. "Beverly, what's your favorite breakfast cereal?" "What picture is on the wall behind you?" "Who is holding your left hand?"

   Remember this process is intended to encourage people to accept and share the everyday flow of feelings in their lives. The support group should not attempt to become a therapy session. Care should be given to use focus time wisely, for dealing with manageable issues, and not ones concerned with deep psychological trauma. The group cannot and must not attempt to take on the responsibility of a professional counselor.

Values

INDIVIDUALLY:

Write a letter in your journal to a personal hero or heroine, or person you admire. Explain what that person stands for in your eyes. What values do you feel you share? Tell about an incident or an overall behavior that demonstrates how you act to support your mutual value. What new behavior or actions are you working toward developing as part of your stand on your value?

IN THE FAMILY, THE CLASSROOM, OR THE SUPPORT GROUP:

1. Not all choices are between good and bad; some are between bad and worse. What is terrible for one person may not be a problem for another. Have the group brainstorm routine family chores. Working from that list, have members make their own personal list, in the order of each chore's distastefulness; then share, either in pairs or with the whole group, how people have rated the chores.[5]

2. External circumstances often affect our values. Working with a partner, list three ways you like to use your spare time. If you inherited a million dollars tomorrow, how would your list change? If you were in an accident and broke both legs, what would you do with your time? If you knew you had only six months to live, how would your time be spent? Share your answers with your partner.

3. Discuss what has the greatest effect on how people value time.

---

[5] Adapted from Leland W. Howe and Mary Martha Howe, "Forced Choice Ladder," in *Personalizing Education, Values Clarification and Beyond* (New York: Hart Publishing Co., 1975), pp. 98–111.

　　　　　　　　　　　　　　EXERCISES AND CLARIFYING TOOLS

I'D RATHER . . . . . . LIST

BEST
_____

fold wash

dry dishes

wash dishes

collect trash

cut lawn

scrub floors

clean toilets

scoop up dog dirt
_____
WORST

Setting Positive Limits

PERSONAL CREDO

Each person brings a personal credo to the process of rule making
—some basic dos and don'ts based on assimilated values of good
and bad behavior. These internalized notions about truthfulness,
humility, loyalty, industriousness, etc., take form in the expectations
we place on ourselves and others. Although we may rarely express
them verbally, these concepts define our personal view of what people must always or never do. They are a basic factor in the kind of
rules that we establish. The following exercise brings out some of
these assumptions for re-examination. In them may lie valuable personal truths to be shared, or rigid biases that promote conflict.

PERSONAL CREDO
In this family (class, group) people should:

ALWAYS	NEVER
1. _____	1. _____
2. _____	2. _____

(list a total of ten)

Using the credo:

INDIVIDUALLY:

1. Fill in the list.
2. Review the list, putting a check next to the beliefs that are supported by your present life style, and putting an X next to those that present a frequent source of conflict.
3. Choose one of the beliefs in the credo that you could proudly hang as a motto over your front door. Think of an incident in your life that typifies this belief. Who was involved? What was your reaction at the time? Write a brief description of the incident and include it, along with the credo, in your journal.

IN THE FAMILY OR THE CLASSROOM:

1. Explain that you want to discuss the kinds of behavior that people admire or are displeased by most. Point out that people have different ideas and attitudes: For instance, some people believe that if you play a game you should always give your all to winning, while others believe that you should never make winning more important than the fun of playing.
2. Ask the group to think quietly for a moment about their shoulds and shouldn'ts. Have the group brainstorm rules, and record them on two large sheets of paper, headed "Always" and "Never." After one is listed, the contributor should state its obverse on the opposite list: "Never scream" may become "Always speak respectfully." The group can help but should not record the counterpart unless the contributor agrees that it accurately represents his thinking.
3. Drawing from the lists, have the group develop a family or class credo stated in the positive. Post it in a prominent place.

IN THE SUPPORT GROUP:

Take five minutes for group members to fill out their "Always" and "Never" lists (as these terms apply to their personal values). Have each person choose one belief and explain to a partner why it is important, describing under what circumstances he would or could compromise or negotiate that belief.

Problem Solving and Conflict Resolution

Teaching the *process* of problem solving has a different goal from using it to solve actual problems. While it is acceptable and often helpful to use the personal problems of workshop or support-group members to examine a method, the only problems that can be resolved during such a session are those that fall under the category of "You Own," or "We Own," the issues. The owners, or in the case of a relationship-owned conflict both parties, must be present. Understanding this distinction and making it clear to the participants can be essential to the success of a session. The teaching and learning process is not to be confused with the involvement with solutions as the final goal.

WARM-UP EXERCISES: QUICK DECISION MAKING

Reflecting the manner in which most of our decisions are made—quickly, on the spur of the moment—these exercises may give insight into the variety of diverse, imaginative solutions that are possible:

- You have just paid for the groceries and are on the way out, when your five-year-old joins you with an opened bag of candy that you did not purchase.
- You are a junior-high-school teacher, walking down the school corridor. Just ahead you see what appears to be a "shake-down" of a seventh grader by two ninth graders.
- You arrive home from work to find your tools spread all over the front lawn, where your twelve-year-old has been building a tree house.
- It is the last day of school. The valedictorian of the senior class arrives late to class with a can of beer in the pocket of her overcoat.

INDIVIDUALLY:

1. For each statement, write down as many possible solutions as you can think of. Allow yourself only thirty seconds for each. Stimulate your imagination; don't stop to judge.
2. Examine your list. Do you solve problems by active or passive means? Do you gather information? Do you act or react? Have any patterns evolved?

IN THE FAMILY, THE CLASSROOM, OR THE SUPPORT GROUP:

1. Pair off with someone you don't usually make decisions with.
2. Have the leader (facilitator) or a group member explain the process: The leader reads the problem aloud to the entire group. Each pair makes a quick decision and must respond in thirty seconds. Try to encourage agreement between them. After the leader calls time, each pair gives its response; no comments are to be offered at this time. Repeat as often as you wish.
3. In a discussion involving the entire group, welcome comments and explore individual reactions: Could you agree in thirty seconds? Was agreement easier as you got to know your partner? How often do you solve problems in this way?

WARM-UP EXERCISES: COOPERATIVE GAMES[6]

Many noncompetitive games can be used effectively as warm-ups to, or during, problem-solving sessions. As laughter, creativity, and nonverbal skills emerge, erroneous preconceptions—that resolving problems need be weighty and ponderous—diminish. Games such as Machine (in which one person making a sound and motion is joined by others in the group, with their own sounds and motions, until all together form a machine) or Pretzel (in which part of the group joins hands in a circle, twists themselves into a pretzel, and must be undone by one or more untwisters) draw a group together in body, spirit, and good humor and prepare them to tackle more serious problems.

EXERCISES FOR TEACHING THE PROBLEM-SOLVING PROCESS: CLAIMING PROBLEMS

The following list of problems is meant to provide an objective starting point for examination of whose unmet needs must be addressed. Remember that there are no right or wrong answers—your perception of a need might well determine how you define whose problem it is.

---

[6] For books on cooperative games, see the Annotated Bibliography, pp. 174, 176.

- You have arranged to visit your parents' home for Thanksgiving dinner. Your spouse, who's announced that he/she's ready to leave, is wearing jeans, a sweatshirt, and sneakers.
- You return from work to find that your fourteen-year-old has used your make-up/shaving equipment without your permission, and it is strewn all over the bathroom.
- You overhear two fellow teachers making disparaging remarks about a student whom you have spent much time with, trying to improve his/her self-image.
- Your two children, aged four and seven, begin quarreling in the back seat of the neighbor's car. You and the neighbor are in the front seat.
- Your spouse reveals an eight-hundred-dollar gambling debt, in front of your father.
- Your nine-year-old comes into the house on a cold, rainy day, with no shoes on, walks past you, and sneezes.
- You have custody of your sixteen-year-old. Your "ex" promises the sixteen-year-old a new MG for his/her birthday.

INDIVIDUALLY:

1. Decide whose problem it is. What needs are involved?
2. Are there any patterns in your responses? Do you automatically assume responsibility for a child's or student's problem? Do you respond differently when the problem involves your spouse? Is your response affected by the presence of a third party?
3. In your journal: a. identify a pattern or insight you have had about your response to problems; b. examine one of your current problems to determine ownership and needs; c. is it more difficult for you to own a problem or to give one up? Why?

IN THE FAMILY, THE CLASSROOM, OR THE SUPPORT GROUP:

1. Explain the theory of problem ownership.
2. Divide into small groups of twos, threes, or fours. Pass out a few problems to each small group. Allowing two to three minutes per problem, have each group try to come to consensus on who owns the problem and what needs are being expressed.
3. Report the experience to the larger group: Discuss the specific problem, who owns it, and the unmet needs that caused it; record the results.

4. Alternative: Have a few group members role play or use puppets to present an example from the list. After the situation is acted out and the problem presented, the whole group then discusses it to determine ownership and needs.

Problem-Solving Methods

The following processes can be used in the various kinds of problem situations: "Turn-Around" Problem Solving helps you to clarify needs when the problem is yours alone; Goal-Wish Problem Solving can be used when the problem belongs to another person; Supportive Presence and Virginia Reel can be used when two people have the problem jointly—when it belongs to their relationship. To teach these processes in groups, we suggest that they be first explained by the leader; then, with either a hypothetical or a volunteered problem, be worked through by the group. In Goal Wish, for example, the whole group works on the problem with the owner. The other processes can be role played for demonstration purposes. The steps to the process should be posted prominently and copies of the steps given to the participants to take home.

"TURN-AROUND" PROBLEM SOLVING

1. DEFINE YOUR ROLE IN THE PROBLEM. Describe the incident or interaction that is troublesome. Describe your behavior and how that pattern of acting affects you. Do you get some reward for acting that way? Or, what price do you pay?
2. IDENTIFY THE FEELINGS INVOLVED. What do you feel when this situation comes up? Can you think of a similar situation when you have reacted in this way? What does it remind you of? (Be on the lookout for loaded words: shy, weak, diminished, should, etc.)
3. EXPLORE HOW YOU MIGHT BE NEGATING YOURSELF. In what ways are you discrediting your own abilities or needs in this situation? Are you making comparisons or assumptions that have led to illogical conclusions? If appropriate, allow yourself to laugh, cry, or let out the feelings in some physical way.

4. TURN AROUND THE NEGATION. Adopt, or "try on," the reverse of the feelings that you discovered in item 3. Turn the invalidation completely around: affirm yourself.

5. TAKE THE FIRST STEP. Decide on one step that you can take that will demonstrate your new assumption about yourself. What do you need to do to accomplish it? When will you do it?

GOAL-WISH PROBLEM SOLVING[7]

Before starting, the group must agree on these points:

- One person will own the problem, and the rest of the group will be used as a "brain trust" to help solve it.

- The other members of the group will not criticize or question the person whose problem is being worked on, except to clarify information.

- No one in the group will criticize or discuss anyone else's ideas.

1. EXPLAIN THE PROBLEM. The owner describes in about three minutes:

> How is this situation a problem?

> Why is it a problem for you rather than for other people?

> What ideas have you already considered that might solve the problem?

> Is there a solution perhaps arrived at through fantasy which, if it came true, would fulfill your dreams?

During this time others in the group should record their thoughts about how the problem might be solved.

The facilitator asks the owner to state the question that she would most like the group to work on. The owner tries to define it using only one phrase, starting with "how to" with an active verb. The facilitator writes this question (and every subsequent one) on a large sheet of paper.

2. GOAL WISH TO FIND ALTERNATIVE SOLUTIONS. The group as a

---

[7] This process is based in part on our own interpretation of some of the principles developed by Synectics, Inc., Cambridge Mass., and Open Connections, Bala Cynwyd, Pa. An additional resource is a book written by the founder of Synectics, Inc., George M. Prince, called *The Practice of Creativity* (New York: Harper & Row, 1970).

whole, including the owner, offers goal wishes in "how to" form. These might prompt unexpected responses. Crazy, unthinkable thoughts often comprise ideas that may have the germ of a possible solution which our usual, more structured thinking might censor.

3. MAKE A SPECIFIED RESPONSE TO SELECT FEASIBLE ALTERNATIVES. The facilitator asks the owner to select those ideas that seem particularly attractive as solutions, and to respond to one of them with a "specified response." (A specified response is made by naming at least three things that are exciting about the idea, by explaining why they are attractive, and by identifying one defect that might need to be remedied in order for the idea to become a viable solution.) The facilitator records these suggestions on a "balance sheet," with the assets on one side and the flaw on the other. The owner formulates a "how to" question about the flaw, so that that idea, too, may become a possible solution to the problem.

4. GOAL WISH TO DETERMINE POSSIBLE COURSES OF ACTION. Again employing the "how to" form, the group brainstorms possible solutions or ways that this goal wish might be accomplished.

5. MAKE A SPECIFIED RESPONSE TO CLARIFY CONSIDERED SOLUTIONS. The owner comments on any ideas that may lead to possible solutions and explores them with the group, using "specified responses," until one or more possibilities are found that the owner believes can be implemented. Having more than one alternative is preferable so that the owner does not feel locked into one solution that may prove to be unacceptable.

6. DETERMINE THE STEPS TO TAKE. The facilitator asks the owner to state the concrete steps that she will take to implement the solution, and to set some goals about when (tomorrow, next week) she will take these steps.

7. CLOSING THE SESSION. The facilitator gives the owner the sheets listing the suggestions for solutions and specified responses. The owner may want to ask some participants afterward for information that was interesting but undiscussed during the session because of the pressure of time.

SUPPORTIVE PRESENCE

1. EXPLAIN THAT YOU ARE THERE TO SEE THAT NEITHER PARTY HURTS THE OTHER WITH WORDS OR DEEDS. Assure those in conflict that their

feelings themselves—all feelings—are acceptable. Acting on them in a way that is hurtful is to be discouraged. If the tension is high, you might suggest that they take time out for releasing their pent-up emotions in a safe way: pounding a pillow, running once around the building, drawing an angry picture.

2. ASSURE THEM THAT THEY CAN WORK THE PROBLEM OUT THEMSELVES. Accompany them to a quiet place and explain that you will remain there to make sure that no one gets hurt. State clearly and simply that you expect them to work out the issue between themselves.

3. SIT DOWN AND WAIT. You might find it helpful to read, or otherwise occupy yourself while you are waiting. Try to remember, though, that your presence is intended to reinforce the belief that those owning the problem *can* solve it without your help. This step may be the most difficult for you and for the others. We are all conditioned to assume that age knows best. Young people may need to test your belief in them by continued requests for assistance or intervention, or by intermittent refusals to negotiate together. The tendency to urge, persuade, coerce, or encourage may be strong. Don't succumb! Once young people realize that resolutions rest with them, they will move ahead themselves. As with Attentive Listening, voluntary silence can be a challenging, illuminating experience.

4. WHEN A RESOLUTION IS REACHED, DO NOT INTERFERE OR PASS JUDGMENT. This is a learning experience, a discovery of the intricacies of fairness and reconciliation; each of which is an aspect of the responsibility for one's relationships. Praise or criticism will imply a lack of faith, so it is best to make no comment on results, unless it is to emphasize trust: "I knew you could do it." Even if you feel that one of the parties is being cheated or manipulated, the important fact is that whatever the resolution, *it has been reached and agreed to by those who own it.* (If you must deal with patterns of manipulation, do so in another, *separate* context.)

VIRGINIA REEL: A AND B OWN THE PROBLEM

1. A talks with C, describing the problem as it affects her. B and D listen without comment.
2. C paraphrases A's statement, with any necessary clarification from A. Again B and D listen.
3. B talks with D, describing the problem as it affects him. A and C listen without comment.
4. D paraphrases B's statement, with any necessary clarification from B. Again A and C listen.
5. A and B continue the dialogue based on the information that has been shared. C and D listen thoughtfully and offer clarification when and if appropriate.

This method can be reciprocal: C and D, in turn, may share their problem, with the assistance of A and B. The advantage of this arrangement is that it settles any sense of indebtedness.

Annotated Bibliography

While there are many books available on building relationships—especially on parenting—those in the following bibliography, annotated by Penni Eldredge-Martin, are particularly recommended, because they provide added dimension to the philosophy and approach of the Nonviolence and Children Program's parent support work. They are straightforward, "hands-on" books that we found readable, stimulating, and encouraging.

The Boston Women's Health Book Collective. *Ourselves and Our Children: A Book by and for Parents.* New York: Random House, 1978.

Writing as parents rather than as professionals, the authors have endeavored, through the informal tone of this manual as well as the anecdotal content, to encourage parents to believe in their ability to help themselves, particularly through reflectiveness, openness, dialogue with other parents, and, most important, learning the ability to ask others for help. For these reasons, the book is intended as a resource throughout the on-going process of parenting.

Appreciating their experiences of working collectively on *Our Bodies, Ourselves,* the ten female authors explain that they chose again to work as a women's collective on this subject, for they felt that the validity of their explorations into the issue of parenting arose from their common experiences as women: as nurturers who had provided daily care and who had been parented primarily by women. At the same time, they add that the decision to examine "parenting" rather than "mothering" is an attempt to shatter the myth that only women can raise children.

We believe that the dissolution of this myth will come about faster, though not necessarily with more ease, if men are involved from the outset. Women *and* men are responsible for the myths of parenting—their creation and their dissolution. As long as women alone discuss, come to understandings, and ask questions about parenting, they may, as the authors say, "grind the lens," but they may simultaneously affix unconscious blinders. Formulating the questions must be as crucial as supplying the responses. Parenting is a process of both "mothering" and "fathering"; to consider it as less cheats all of us—mothers, fathers, and children. The extended bibliography and resource lists are highly recommended.

Boulding, Elise. *The Personhood of Children.* Philadelphia: Religious Education Committee of Friends General Conference, 1975. (Available from the above at 1501 Cherry Street, Philadelphia, Pa. 19102; $1.50.)

Adult-child relationships outside the family build self-confidence and competence, and offer children creative social roles, while providing adults with much-needed fresh perspective on their activities. These interactions can ease the complex, overburdened parent-child relationships of our age-graded society. Boulding emphasizes that while adults should not isolate children by age-grading them, "to pretend that young people 'know as much as we do' when in fact they don't is hypocrisy [p. 6]." Rather than accepting that children experientially know as much as adults, we must seek our own capacities and responsibilities, respect their resources of enthusiasm, abundant energy, and creativity, and acknowledge the ability of each to build serious relationships from a recognition of mutual interests.

Carmichael, Carrie. *Non-Sexist Childraising.* Boston: Beacon Press, 1977.

Through talking with psychiatrists, pediatricians, psychologists, and many, many parents, Carmichael has assessed the experiences of those trying to encourage children to define themselves according to personality instead of sex. She believes that the best way to do so is to live one's personal life in a nonsexist manner, but when this is not possible, at least talk about the oppression and stereotyping that occur in society because of one's sex.

Nonsexist childraising is happening in many ways, as seen by the information gathered here. There are no guidelines, and the results are still to be tabulated, as this generation has not yet matured. Nonjudgmental throughout, Carmichael stresses the importance and difficulty of attempting to integrate and live fully one's feminist beliefs.

The Ecumenical Task Force on Christian Education for World Peace. *Try This: Family Adventures Toward Shalom.* Nashville, Tenn.: Discipleship Resources, 1979.

Easily adapted for intergenerational use, this family-activity workbook encourages all ages to share the values of, and to develop the skills necessary to pursue, a peace-oriented lifestyle, valuing all people, using conflict creatively, participating in the creative change of institutions and systems that would make the goal more attainable, caring for and sharing world resources, and choosing to live joyously. The basic assumptions supporting the activities are twofold: first, that responsible action and understanding spring from shared experiences of and reflection upon new ideas, attitudes, and behaviors; and, secondly, that through this examination of our own lives and families we are strengthened to develop responsibly, assertively, and creatively, and to enter into dialogue and action on larger human issues, such as human rights, war and peace, sharing of world resources, disarmament, etc.

Faber, Adele, and Mazlish, Elaine. *Liberated Parents/Liberated Children.* New York: Grosset & Dunlap, 1974.

Faber and Mazlish participated in an ongoing parent workshop led by Dr. Haim Ginott, and this warm, delightful book follows their experiences both as workshop participants and as family members anxious to apply new, exciting insights. By sharing with the reader not only their hopes and successes but also their misgivings and relapses, they trace the reality of affirmative growth and change, while demonstrating the power and resiliency of supportive relationships.

Gaylin, Willard. *Feelings: Our Vital Signs.* New York: Harper & Row, 1979.

Gaylin believes that feelings are "instruments of rationality, not—as some would have it—alternatives to it." Drawing skillfully and enticingly from classic and contemporary literature, he illustrates the commonalities and qualitative differences within our broad range of feelings. This book does much to enrich and clarify our "vocabulary" of feelings, and to promote an appreciation of feelings as vitalizing and coping resources. The chapter on feeling proud underscores the need for and propriety of affirmation—especially self-affirmation!

Gordon, Thomas, with Judith Gordon Sands, *P.E.T. in Action.* New York: Bantam Books, 1978.

In this re-evaluation of his original concepts, Gordon clearly shares what he has learned from PET instructors and parents over the years. The development of his theory, based on subsequent experiences, provides an excellent example of the ongoing nature of the change and adaptability that are necessary in keeping any theory current, and that are imperative for effective parenting.

The I-Message is expanded beyond its original definition as merely an effective means of influencing children's unacceptable behavior. Gordon questions the use of praise as a mode of child modification, as it often communicates that the recipient is inferior to the sender.

In a chapter on values, Gordon suggests that modeling, being an effective consultant, accepting what you can't change, and re-examination of one's own beliefs are helpful when confronted with a clash over values. We, on the other hand, feel that these four concepts are central in all areas of parenting. Gordon's inclusion of them in only one final chapter seems to downplay their importance. Parents can easily accept and use the various techniques of PET (I-Messages, Active Listening, No-Lose Problem Solving) without ever incorporating these four concepts or understanding their relation to the techniques. Techniques can easily be used "on" others, whereas practicing the concepts requires hard work and involvement of the whole person in the context of a personal and vital relationship.

Greenberg, Selma. *Right from the Start: A Guide to Nonsexist Child Rearing.* Boston: Houghton Mifflin Co., 1979.

Arguing that nonsexist childraising must counter three major myths—"the myth of the opposite sex, the myth of the male as the real human being, and the myth of the male as the sexual being" (p. 227)—Selma Greenberg asserts that sexist notions and practices are best challenged from the very beginning at the child's birth, but she also recognizes that many families no longer have this option. Her text meets the needs of all families by making hypotheses accessible through theoretical discussions of and simple, practical suggestions to interrupt stereotypical family power structures, parent roles, toys, language, behavior, and schooling, to list a few.

Throughout, adults, particularly mothers and fathers, are urged to practice their nonsexist beliefs responsibly: mothers must have assertive physical and psychological excursions with their infants and toddlers beyond the home; fathers must enter into caretaking roles, not only with their young children, but with their homes and wives. Parents must determine and *teach* acceptable behavior and values to their children, and boys and girls must be welcomed into the family as members with equal rights and growing responsibilities to themselves, each other, and the family.

This hopeful, exciting discussion does not promise easy answers but encourages responsible authentic relationships between men and women, as well as between parents and children.

Haessly, Jacqueline. *Peacemaking: Family Activities for Justice and Peace*. New York: Paulist Press, 1980.

In our complex society, how do we nurture children in a way that ensures their physical, spiritual, emotional, and moral development? Can we help our children develop both the awareness and the skills necessary to be creative, just people? With these questions in mind, Haessly envisions the family circle as capable of becoming a safe, secure place, in which all members share insights and fears, risk new ideas, and even fail.

The booklet is divided into two parts: in the first are discussed the four steppingstones to peace (affirmation, respect for differences, cooperation, and the use of creative means to resolve conflict); the global village and the concepts of interdependence, stewardship, and celebration are explained in the second. Each chapter covers basic principles, offers specific activities around the theme, and ends with a prayer or celebration. It expresses the goal that through such family experiences, individuals will be strengthened to move singly and in groups to affect change in their worlds.

While activities are intended primarily for the family, they can easily be adapted for use in other intergenerational settings.

Howell, Mary C. *Helping Ourselves: Families and the Human Network*. Boston: Beacon Press, 1975.

Mary Howell's experiences as a practicing physician have led her to insist that when people have enough information, adequate time, support, and reassurance to reach decisions about family problems, they usually come to solutions that respect the needs of individual members and enhance the group's welfare. For these reasons, she seeks fundamental changes, when necessary, in the relationships among families, communities, and professionals that would assure these conditions.

Although many of the suggestions are exciting and feasible, the perspective is distinctly oriented toward urban communities. Implementation would be difficult, if at all possible, in rural areas.

Jackins, Harvey. *The Human Side of Human Beings: The Theory of Re-Evaluation Counseling*. Seattle, Wash.: Rational Island Publishers, 1965 (P.O. Box 2081, Main Office Station, Seattle, Wash. 98111).

Written as an introductory text for Re-Evaluation Counseling, this short, theoretical study postulates some provocative concepts concerning human nature. Jackins defines the goals of human nature as vast intelligence, zestful enjoyment of living and loving, cooperative relationships with others. The failure to fulfill these potentials, he asserts, is the result of our susceptibility to having these essentials damaged and limited by physical and emotional traumas. These simply stated concepts have complex, wide-ranging ramifications.

Judson, Stephanie, ed. *A Manual on Nonviolence and Children*. Philadelphia: Philadelphia Yearly Meeting, Peace Committee, 1977.

Predecessor to our current text, this hands-on manual describes the Nonviolence and Children Program's early work in elementary schools with children and teachers. Activities, agendas, anecdotes, and skills are discussed within the theoretical framework of affirmation, sharing, a supportive community, the resolution of conflict, and the celebration of life.

The clear, simple explanations and the format (softbound with illustrations), comments, and results reported by those who have used the skills make the material readily available and helpful to the classroom teacher. An annotated list of children's books, as well as an appendix containing the cooperative-games booklet *For the Fun of It,* are excellent resources.

Included are discussions of the early thought and agenda of parent support groups. It is significant to note how the theory has evolved and expanded in the last seven years.

Montessori, Maria. *The Child in the Family.* New York: Avon Books, 1970.

Montessori, in reverent, simple language, recognizes our responsibility, as adults, to that "spiritual embryo" that confronts us in each child. Writing to describe the theory upon which her schools are based, she encourages respect and understanding for children's activities, rather than the usual intervention, which suppresses not only a child's natural spontaneity, but also his will and independence. Of her many powerful beliefs, two are particularly appropriate to this book. First, contrary to the way adults usually see it, children themselves actually teach love. Second, we should let go of our expectations of perfection and allow ourselves to learn from our children, who are still willing and ready to love us when we err and apologize. Children, as she sees them, are naturals at giving permission.

Orlick, Terry. *The Cooperative Sports and Games Book: Challenge without Competition.* New York: Pantheon Books, 1978.

With more than one hundred cooperative games for people of all ages, including some from other cultures, gaming foundations, parents, educators, and many created by the author himself, the goals emerge as simple, yet profound: Through the four components of cooperative games—cooperation, acceptance, involvement, and fun—we can have fun as we learn positive things about ourselves and how we can behave in the world at large.

Particularly helpful is a description of semi-cooperative adult games adapted from such sports as basketball and volleyball, evaluative techniques for those embarking on the use of cooperative games for the first time, and a discussion of creating your own games, along with a few examples.

Rogers, Carl. *On Becoming a Person: A Therapist's View of Psychotherapy.* Boston: Houghton Mifflin Co., 1961.

A compilation of articles by Carl Rogers with the recurring theme of improving relationships.

Especially encouraged are those that seek to understand and share the integrity of each person's feelings and needs, with an ultimate goal of freedom for each one to grow. This mutual growth rests upon being dependably real, communicating unambiguously, finding the strength and inner security to be separate from the other, keeping the relationship free of evaluations or judgments, acting sensitively, and always meeting this other as a person in the process of becoming.

Satir, Virginia. *Peoplemaking.* Palo Alto, Calif. Science & Behavior Books, 1972.

With a knack for clear, pointed analogies throughout, Satir likens the family to a "factory," one in which physically healthy, mentally alert, feeling, loving, playful, authentic, creative, productive human beings are made. The four bases upon which this production depends are self-worth, communication, rules, and links to society.

There is an optimistic, wholesome quality to the text, which is enhanced by simple line drawings, exercises that stress the physical expression of feelings, and the oft-repeated belief that there is hope that anything can change. A particularly helpful contribution is the consideration of single parents, "blended" and foster families, and the unfortunate disregard of resources resulting from the stereotyping of older people.

Simon, Sidney B., Howe, Leland W., and Kirschenbaum, Howard. *Values Clarification: A Handbook of Practical Strategies for Teachers and Students.* New York: Hart Publishing Co., 1972.

Though written for classroom use, the values clarification strategies in this book are applicable and useful for group and individual use. Included are an excellent brief explanation of the values clarification approach and descriptions of some basic evaluative and thought-stretching mechanisms, such as Brainstorming, Alternatives Search, Consequences Search, and others. More than just strategies, these tools illustrate a method of objectifying situations for clearer analysis and more creative responses.

Simon, Sidney B., and Olds, Sally Wendkos. *Helping Your Child Learn Right from Wrong: A*

Guide to Values Clarification. New York: Mc-Graw-Hill Book Co., 1977.

This concise, simply written book makes a great sourcebook for teaching the family's values through activities that provide growth and enjoyment. Especially useful in outlining the processes of values clarification are the Fourteen Guidelines for Parents, which recommend the continuing process of evaluating and defining standards, encourage setting a nonintimidating setting in which children can work on their values, and emphasize the benefits of nonmanipulation. Also excellent are the Seven Ground Rules for Everyone, a code to protect the rights, sensitivities, and participation of all parties.

The authors state that the three M's—moralizing, manipulating, and modeling—do not "work any more." This statement, however, seems misleading. Clearly these behaviors do affect and teach children about adult values, though they may not always do so in a positive way. We all need to remain aware of how we *do* moralize, manipulate, and model as we act on our own values, and need to be carefully attuned to whether we do so in a moral and productive fashion.

Winn, Marie. *The Plug-In Drug.* New York: Viking Press, 1977.

TV a drug? Yes! exclaims Marie Winn in a sensitive and revolutionary look at this pervasive institution. Television has become a drug administered to children by adults in search of relief. Complex results, gathered from families and professionals across the country, include the failure to develop vocabulary or commitment to the concept of human sensitivity, parental withdrawal from the active socialization of children, and the individual family's loss of its unique identity, as television becomes a common denominator in family life.

In a supportive, affirming, yet challenging text for parents, Winn acknowledges the inherent difficulty in balancing the needs of parents and children within the family setting. Alternatives and suggestions, both successful and unsuccessful, are shared from the childraising experiences of pre- and post-TV families.

About the Author

Lois Dorn was co-coordinator of the Nonviolence and Children Program of the Society of Friends in Philadelphia from 1976 until 1980. During that time she conducted numerous school, parent, and intergenerational workshops, out of which came many of the experiences described in this book. She is a founding member of a parent-owned, cooperative school for preschool through the eighth grade in Fort Washington, Pennsylvania. She is currently working with the Juvenile Justice Center in Philadelphia and on a project of the Abington Peacemakers to help adults work with children on their fears of nuclear disaster.

A native of Philadelphia, Lois Dorn lives in Jenkintown, Pennsylvania, with her husband and three sons.

The Nonviolence and Children Program continues to run parenting and teaching workshops and training programs along the East Coast, and there are sister programs among Friends' organizations throughout the country. For more information, write to the Nonviolence and Children Program, Friends Peace Committee, 1515 Cherry Street, Philadelphia, Pa. 19102.